Address ______________________ Price ______________

Bedrooms ________ Bathrooms ________ Sq.Ft. ______________

Lot Size: ________ Year Built ________ School District ________

Annual Tax ________

EXTERIOR

	Good	Average	Poor
View/Yard/Landscaping	☐	☐	☐
Trees	☐	☐	☐
Lawn (Front)	☐	☐	☐
Lawn (Back)	☐	☐	☐
Fences (condition)	☐	☐	☐
Landscaping (condition)	☐	☐	☐
Irrigation / Sprinkler	☐	☐	☐
	☐	☐	☐
House Type	☐	☐	☐
Exterior Siding	☐	☐	☐
Deck / Patio / Porch	☐	☐	☐
Garage	☐	☐	☐
Window / Doors	☐	☐	☐
Roof / Gutters	☐	☐	☐
Fencing	☐	☐	☐

HOME SYSTEMS

	Good	Average	Poor
Electrical	☐	☐	☐
Air Conditioning / Fans	☐	☐	☐
Heating	☐	☐	☐
Security	☐	☐	☐
Plumbing	☐	☐	☐
Intercom	☐	☐	☐

FEATURES

	Good	Average	Poor
Home Warranty	☐	☐	☐
Energy Saving Features	☐	☐	☐

INTERIOR

	Good	Average	Poor
Walls / Trim / Ceilings	☐	☐	☐
Flooring	☐	☐	☐
Stairs	☐	☐	☐
Storage	☐	☐	☐
Living Room	☐	☐	☐
Family Room	☐	☐	☐
Dining Room	☐	☐	☐

	Good	Average	Poor
Master Bedroom	☐	☐	☐
Bedroom 2	☐	☐	☐
Bedroom 3	☐	☐	☐
Bedroom 4	☐	☐	☐
Master Bathroom	☐	☐	☐
Bathroom 2	☐	☐	☐
Bathroom 3	☐	☐	☐
Bonus / Game Room	☐	☐	☐

	Good	Average	Poor
Kitchen	☐	☐	☐
Cabinets	☐	☐	☐
Countertop	☐	☐	☐
Counter Space	☐	☐	☐
Flooring	☐	☐	☐
Oven / Stove	☐	☐	☐
Microwave	☐	☐	☐
Layout	☐	☐	☐
Light Fixtures	☐	☐	☐
Backsplash	☐	☐	☐
Pantry	☐	☐	☐
Appliances	☐	☐	☐
Island	☐	☐	☐

	Good	Average	Poor
Basement	☐	☐	☐
Garage	☐	☐	☐

COMMUNITY

	Good	Average	Poor
Immediate Neighborhood	☐	☐	☐
Close to Employment	☐	☐	☐
Close to Shopping	☐	☐	☐
Close to Transportation	☐	☐	☐
Close to Schools / Daycare	☐	☐	☐
Close to Places of Worship	☐	☐	☐
Near Recreational Facilities	☐	☐	☐
Close to Airport	☐	☐	☐
Near Police and Fire Department	☐	☐	☐

Address ______________________ Price ______________

Bedrooms ____________ Bathrooms ____________ Sq.Ft. ______________

Lot Size: ____________ Year Built ____________ School District ________

Annual Tax __________

EXTERIOR

	Good	Average	Poor
View/Yard/Landscaping			
Trees			
Lawn (Front)			
Lawn (Back)			
Fences (condition)			
Landscaping (condition)			
Irrigation / Sprinkler			
House Type			
Exterior Siding			
Deck / Patio / Porch			
Garage			
Window / Doors			
Roof / Gutters			
Fencing			

HOME SYSTEMS

	Good	Average	Poor
Electrical			
Air Conditioning / Fans			
Heating			
Security			
Plumbing			
Intercom			

FEATURES

	Good	Average	Poor
Home Warranty			
Energy Saving Features			

INTERIOR

	Good	Average	Poor
Walls / Trim / Ceilings			
Flooring			
Stairs			
Storage			
Living Room			
Family Room			
Dining Room			

	Good	Average	Poor
Master Bedroom			
Bedroom 2			
Bedroom 3			
Bedroom 4			
Master Bathroom			
Bathroom 2			
Bathroom 3			
Bonus / Game Room			

	Good	Average	Poor
Kitchen			
Cabinets			
Countertop			
Counter Space			
Flooring			
Oven / Stove			
Microwave			
Layout			
Light Fixtures			
Backsplash			
Pantry			
Appliances			
Island			

	Good	Average	Poor
Basement			
Garage			

COMMUNITY

	Good	Average	Poor
Immediate Neighborhood			
Close to Employment			
Close to Shopping			
Close to Transportation			
Close to Schools / Daycare			
Close to Places of Worship			
Near Recreational Facilities			
Close to Airport			
Near Police and Fire Department			

Address ______________________________ Price ______________

Bedrooms __________ Bathrooms ___________ Sq.Ft. ______________

Lot Size: __________ Year Built ____________ School District ________

Annual Tax __________

EXTERIOR

	Good	Average	Poor
View/Yard/Landscaping	☐	☐	☐
Trees	☐	☐	☐
Lawn (Front)	☐	☐	☐
Lawn (Back)	☐	☐	☐
Fences (condition)	☐	☐	☐
Landscaping (condition)	☐	☐	☐
Irrigation / Sprinkler	☐	☐	☐
	☐	☐	☐
House Type	☐	☐	☐
Exterior Siding	☐	☐	☐
Deck / Patio / Porch	☐	☐	☐
Garage	☐	☐	☐
Window / Doors	☐	☐	☐
Roof / Gutters	☐	☐	☐
Fencing	☐	☐	☐

HOME SYSTEMS

	Good	Average	Poor
Electrical	☐	☐	☐
Air Conditioning / Fans	☐	☐	☐
Heating	☐	☐	☐
Security	☐	☐	☐
Plumbing	☐	☐	☐
Intercom	☐	☐	☐

FEATURES

	Good	Average	Poor
Home Warranty	☐	☐	☐
Energy Saving Features	☐	☐	☐

INTERIOR

	Good	Average	Poor
Walls / Trim / Ceilings	☐	☐	☐
Flooring	☐	☐	☐
Stairs	☐	☐	☐
Storage	☐	☐	☐
Living Room	☐	☐	☐
Family Room	☐	☐	☐
Dining Room	☐	☐	☐

	Good	Average	Poor
Master Bedroom	☐	☐	☐
Bedroom 2	☐	☐	☐
Bedroom 3	☐	☐	☐
Bedroom 4	☐	☐	☐
Master Bathroom	☐	☐	☐
Bathroom 2	☐	☐	☐
Bathroom 3	☐	☐	☐
Bonus / Game Room	☐	☐	☐

	Good	Average	Poor
Kitchen	☐	☐	☐
Cabinets	☐	☐	☐
Countertop	☐	☐	☐
Counter Space	☐	☐	☐
Flooring	☐	☐	☐
Oven / Stove	☐	☐	☐
Microwave	☐	☐	☐
Layout	☐	☐	☐
Light Fixtures	☐	☐	☐
Backsplash	☐	☐	☐
Pantry	☐	☐	☐
Appliances	☐	☐	☐
Island	☐	☐	☐

	Good	Average	Poor
Basement	☐	☐	☐
Garage	☐	☐	☐

COMMUNITY

	Good	Average	Poor
Immediate Neighborhood	☐	☐	☐
Close to Employment	☐	☐	☐
Close to Shopping	☐	☐	☐
Close to Transportation	☐	☐	☐
Close to Schools / Daycare	☐	☐	☐
Close to Places of Worship	☐	☐	☐
Near Recreational Facilities	☐	☐	☐
Close to Airport	☐	☐	☐
Near Police and Fire Department	☐	☐	☐

Address ______________________________ Price ______________

Bedrooms __________ Bathrooms __________ Sq.Ft. ______________

Lot Size: __________ Year Built __________ School District _______

Annual Tax __________

EXTERIOR

	Good	Average	Poor
View/Yard/Landscaping	☐	☐	☐
Trees	☐	☐	☐
Lawn (Front)	☐	☐	☐
Lawn (Back)	☐	☐	☐
Fences (condition)	☐	☐	☐
Landscaping (condition)	☐	☐	☐
Irrigation / Sprinkler	☐	☐	☐
	☐	☐	☐
House Type	☐	☐	☐
Exterior Siding	☐	☐	☐
Deck / Patio / Porch	☐	☐	☐
Garage	☐	☐	☐
Window / Doors	☐	☐	☐
Roof / Gutters	☐	☐	☐
Fencing	☐	☐	☐

HOME SYSTEMS

	Good	Average	Poor
Electrical	☐	☐	☐
Air Conditioning / Fans	☐	☐	☐
Heating	☐	☐	☐
Security	☐	☐	☐
Plumbing	☐	☐	☐
Intercom	☐	☐	☐

FEATURES

	Good	Average	Poor
Home Warranty	☐	☐	☐
Energy Saving Features	☐	☐	☐

INTERIOR

	Good	Average	Poor
Walls / Trim / Ceilings	☐	☐	☐
Flooring	☐	☐	☐
Stairs	☐	☐	☐
Storage	☐	☐	☐
Living Room	☐	☐	☐
Family Room	☐	☐	☐
Dining Room	☐	☐	☐

	Good	Average	Poor
Master Bedroom	☐	☐	☐
Bedroom 2	☐	☐	☐
Bedroom 3	☐	☐	☐
Bedroom 4	☐	☐	☐
Master Bathroom	☐	☐	☐
Bathroom 2	☐	☐	☐
Bathroom 3	☐	☐	☐
Bonus / Game Room	☐	☐	☐

	Good	Average	Poor
Kitchen	☐	☐	☐
Cabinets	☐	☐	☐
Countertop	☐	☐	☐
Counter Space	☐	☐	☐
Flooring	☐	☐	☐
Oven / Stove	☐	☐	☐
Microwave	☐	☐	☐
Layout	☐	☐	☐
Light Fixtures	☐	☐	☐
Backsplash	☐	☐	☐
Pantry	☐	☐	☐
Appliances	☐	☐	☐
Island	☐	☐	☐

	Good	Average	Poor
Basement	☐	☐	☐
Garage	☐	☐	☐

COMMUNITY

	Good	Average	Poor
Immediate Neighborhood	☐	☐	☐
Close to Employment	☐	☐	☐
Close to Shopping	☐	☐	☐
Close to Transportation	☐	☐	☐
Close to Schools / Daycare	☐	☐	☐
Close to Places of Worship	☐	☐	☐
Near Recreational Facilities	☐	☐	☐
Close to Airport	☐	☐	☐
Near Police and Fire Department	☐	☐	☐

Address ____________________ Price ____________

Bedrooms __________ Bathrooms __________ Sq.Ft. ____________

Lot Size: __________ Year Built __________ School District ________

Annual Tax __________

EXTERIOR

	Good	Average	Poor
View/Yard/Landscaping	☐	☐	☐
Trees	☐	☐	☐
Lawn (Front)	☐	☐	☐
Lawn (Back)	☐	☐	☐
Fences (condition)	☐	☐	☐
Landscaping (condition)	☐	☐	☐
Irrigation / Sprinkler	☐	☐	☐
	☐	☐	☐
House Type	☐	☐	☐
Exterior Siding	☐	☐	☐
Deck / Patio / Porch	☐	☐	☐
Garage	☐	☐	☐
Window / Doors	☐	☐	☐
Roof / Gutters	☐	☐	☐
Fencing	☐	☐	☐

HOME SYSTEMS

	Good	Average	Poor
Electrical	☐	☐	☐
Air Conditioning / Fans	☐	☐	☐
Heating	☐	☐	☐
Security	☐	☐	☐
Plumbing	☐	☐	☐
Intercom	☐	☐	☐

FEATURES

	Good	Average	Poor
Home Warranty	☐	☐	☐
Energy Saving Features	☐	☐	☐

INTERIOR

	Good	Average	Poor
Walls / Trim / Ceilings	☐	☐	☐
Flooring	☐	☐	☐
Stairs	☐	☐	☐
Storage	☐	☐	☐
Living Room	☐	☐	☐
Family Room	☐	☐	☐
Dining Room	☐	☐	☐

	Good	Average	Poor
Master Bedroom	☐	☐	☐
Bedroom 2	☐	☐	☐
Bedroom 3	☐	☐	☐
Bedroom 4	☐	☐	☐
Master Bathroom	☐	☐	☐
Bathroom 2	☐	☐	☐
Bathroom 3	☐	☐	☐
Bonus / Game Room	☐	☐	☐

	Good	Average	Poor
Kitchen	☐	☐	☐
Cabinets	☐	☐	☐
Countertop	☐	☐	☐
Counter Space	☐	☐	☐
Flooring	☐	☐	☐
Oven / Stove	☐	☐	☐
Microwave	☐	☐	☐
Layout	☐	☐	☐
Light Fixtures	☐	☐	☐
Backsplash	☐	☐	☐
Pantry	☐	☐	☐
Appliances	☐	☐	☐
Island	☐	☐	☐

	Good	Average	Poor
Basement	☐	☐	☐
Garage	☐	☐	☐

COMMUNITY

	Good	Average	Poor
Immediate Neighborhood	☐	☐	☐
Close to Employment	☐	☐	☐
Close to Shopping	☐	☐	☐
Close to Transportation	☐	☐	☐
Close to Schools / Daycare	☐	☐	☐
Close to Places of Worship	☐	☐	☐
Near Recreational Facilities	☐	☐	☐
Close to Airport	☐	☐	☐
Near Police and Fire Department	☐	☐	☐

Address ______________________ Price ____________

Bedrooms ____________ Bathrooms ____________ Sq.Ft. ____________

Lot Size: ____________ Year Built ____________ School District ________

Annual Tax ____________

EXTERIOR

	Good	Average	Poor
View/Yard/Landscaping	☐	☐	☐
Trees	☐	☐	☐
Lawn (Front)	☐	☐	☐
Lawn (Back)	☐	☐	☐
Fences (condition)	☐	☐	☐
Landscaping (condition)	☐	☐	☐
Irrigation / Sprinkler	☐	☐	☐
	☐	☐	☐
House Type	☐	☐	☐
Exterior Siding	☐	☐	☐
Deck / Patio / Porch	☐	☐	☐
Garage	☐	☐	☐
Window / Doors	☐	☐	☐
Roof / Gutters	☐	☐	☐
Fencing	☐	☐	☐

HOME SYSTEMS

	Good	Average	Poor
Electrical	☐	☐	☐
Air Conditioning / Fans	☐	☐	☐
Heating	☐	☐	☐
Security	☐	☐	☐
Plumbing	☐	☐	☐
Intercom	☐	☐	☐

FEATURES

	Good	Average	Poor
Home Warranty	☐	☐	☐
Energy Saving Features	☐	☐	☐

INTERIOR

	Good	Average	Poor
Walls / Trim / Ceilings	☐	☐	☐
Flooring	☐	☐	☐
Stairs	☐	☐	☐
Storage	☐	☐	☐
Living Room	☐	☐	☐
Family Room	☐	☐	☐
Dining Room	☐	☐	☐

	Good	Average	Poor
Master Bedroom	☐	☐	☐
Bedroom 2	☐	☐	☐
Bedroom 3	☐	☐	☐
Bedroom 4	☐	☐	☐
Master Bathroom	☐	☐	☐
Bathroom 2	☐	☐	☐
Bathroom 3	☐	☐	☐
Bonus / Game Room	☐	☐	☐

	Good	Average	Poor
Kitchen	☐	☐	☐
Cabinets	☐	☐	☐
Countertop	☐	☐	☐
Counter Space	☐	☐	☐
Flooring	☐	☐	☐
Oven / Stove	☐	☐	☐
Microwave	☐	☐	☐
Layout	☐	☐	☐
Light Fixtures	☐	☐	☐
Backsplash	☐	☐	☐
Pantry	☐	☐	☐
Appliances	☐	☐	☐
Island	☐	☐	☐

	Good	Average	Poor
Basement	☐	☐	☐
Garage	☐	☐	☐

COMMUNITY

	Good	Average	Poor
Immediate Neighborhood	☐	☐	☐
Close to Employment	☐	☐	☐
Close to Shopping	☐	☐	☐
Close to Transportation	☐	☐	☐
Close to Schools / Daycare	☐	☐	☐
Close to Places of Worship	☐	☐	☐
Near Recreational Facilities	☐	☐	☐
Close to Airport	☐	☐	☐
Near Police and Fire Department	☐	☐	☐

Address ______________________ Price ____________

Bedrooms ________ Bathrooms ________ Sq.Ft. ____________

Lot Size: ________ Year Built ________ School District ________

Annual Tax ________

EXTERIOR

	Good	Average	Poor
View/Yard/Landscaping	☐	☐	☐
Trees	☐	☐	☐
Lawn (Front)	☐	☐	☐
Lawn (Back)	☐	☐	☐
Fences (condition)	☐	☐	☐
Landscaping (condition)	☐	☐	☐
Irrigation / Sprinkler	☐	☐	☐
	☐	☐	☐
House Type	☐	☐	☐
Exterior Siding	☐	☐	☐
Deck / Patio / Porch	☐	☐	☐
Garage	☐	☐	☐
Window / Doors	☐	☐	☐
Roof / Gutters	☐	☐	☐
Fencing	☐	☐	☐

HOME SYSTEMS

	Good	Average	Poor
Electrical	☐	☐	☐
Air Conditioning / Fans	☐	☐	☐
Heating	☐	☐	☐
Security	☐	☐	☐
Plumbing	☐	☐	☐
Intercom	☐	☐	☐

FEATURES

	Good	Average	Poor
Home Warranty	☐	☐	☐
Energy Saving Features	☐	☐	☐

INTERIOR

	Good	Average	Poor
Walls / Trim / Ceilings	☐	☐	☐
Flooring	☐	☐	☐
Stairs	☐	☐	☐
Storage	☐	☐	☐
Living Room	☐	☐	☐
Family Room	☐	☐	☐
Dining Room	☐	☐	☐

	Good	Average	Poor
Master Bedroom	☐	☐	☐
Bedroom 2	☐	☐	☐
Bedroom 3	☐	☐	☐
Bedroom 4	☐	☐	☐
Master Bathroom	☐	☐	☐
Bathroom 2	☐	☐	☐
Bathroom 3	☐	☐	☐
Bonus / Game Room	☐	☐	☐

	Good	Average	Poor
Kitchen	☐	☐	☐
Cabinets	☐	☐	☐
Countertop	☐	☐	☐
Counter Space	☐	☐	☐
Flooring	☐	☐	☐
Oven / Stove	☐	☐	☐
Microwave	☐	☐	☐
Layout	☐	☐	☐
Light Fixtures	☐	☐	☐
Backsplash	☐	☐	☐
Pantry	☐	☐	☐
Appliances	☐	☐	☐
Island	☐	☐	☐

	Good	Average	Poor
Basement	☐	☐	☐
Garage	☐	☐	☐

COMMUNITY

	Good	Average	Poor
Immediate Neighborhood	☐	☐	☐
Close to Employment	☐	☐	☐
Close to Shopping	☐	☐	☐
Close to Transportation	☐	☐	☐
Close to Schools / Daycare	☐	☐	☐
Close to Places of Worship	☐	☐	☐
Near Recreational Facilities	☐	☐	☐
Close to Airport	☐	☐	☐
Near Police and Fire Department	☐	☐	☐

Address ______________________ Price ______________

Bedrooms __________ Bathrooms __________ Sq.Ft. ______________

Lot Size: __________ Year Built __________ School District ______

Annual Tax ________

EXTERIOR

	Good	Average	Poor
View/Yard/Landscaping	☐	☐	☐
Trees	☐	☐	☐
Lawn (Front)	☐	☐	☐
Lawn (Back)	☐	☐	☐
Fences (condition)	☐	☐	☐
Landscaping (condition)	☐	☐	☐
Irrigation / Sprinkler	☐	☐	☐
	☐	☐	☐
House Type	☐	☐	☐
Exterior Siding	☐	☐	☐
Deck / Patio / Porch	☐	☐	☐
Garage	☐	☐	☐
Window / Doors	☐	☐	☐
Roof / Gutters	☐	☐	☐
Fencing	☐	☐	☐

HOME SYSTEMS

	Good	Average	Poor
Electrical	☐	☐	☐
Air Conditioning / Fans	☐	☐	☐
Heating	☐	☐	☐
Security	☐	☐	☐
Plumbing	☐	☐	☐
Intercom	☐	☐	☐

FEATURES

	Good	Average	Poor
Home Warranty	☐	☐	☐
Energy Saving Features	☐	☐	☐

INTERIOR

	Good	Average	Poor
Walls / Trim / Ceilings	☐	☐	☐
Flooring	☐	☐	☐
Stairs	☐	☐	☐
Storage	☐	☐	☐
Living Room	☐	☐	☐
Family Room	☐	☐	☐
Dining Room	☐	☐	☐

	Good	Average	Poor
Master Bedroom	☐	☐	☐
Bedroom 2	☐	☐	☐
Bedroom 3	☐	☐	☐
Bedroom 4	☐	☐	☐
Master Bathroom	☐	☐	☐
Bathroom 2	☐	☐	☐
Bathroom 3	☐	☐	☐
Bonus / Game Room	☐	☐	☐

	Good	Average	Poor
Kitchen	☐	☐	☐
Cabinets	☐	☐	☐
Countertop	☐	☐	☐
Counter Space	☐	☐	☐
Flooring	☐	☐	☐
Oven / Stove	☐	☐	☐
Microwave	☐	☐	☐
Layout	☐	☐	☐
Light Fixtures	☐	☐	☐
Backsplash	☐	☐	☐
Pantry	☐	☐	☐
Appliances	☐	☐	☐
Island	☐	☐	☐

	Good	Average	Poor
Basement	☐	☐	☐
Garage	☐	☐	☐

COMMUNITY

	Good	Average	Poor
Immediate Neighborhood	☐	☐	☐
Close to Employment	☐	☐	☐
Close to Shopping	☐	☐	☐
Close to Transportation	☐	☐	☐
Close to Schools / Daycare	☐	☐	☐
Close to Places of Worship	☐	☐	☐
Near Recreational Facilities	☐	☐	☐
Close to Airport	☐	☐	☐
Near Police and Fire Department	☐	☐	☐

Address ______________________________ Price ______________

Bedrooms __________ Bathrooms __________ Sq.Ft. ______________

Lot Size: __________ Year Built __________ School District _______

Annual Tax __________

EXTERIOR

	Good	Average	Poor
View/Yard/Landscaping	☐	☐	☐
Trees	☐	☐	☐
Lawn (Front)	☐	☐	☐
Lawn (Back)	☐	☐	☐
Fences (condition)	☐	☐	☐
Landscaping (condition)	☐	☐	☐
Irrigation / Sprinkler	☐	☐	☐
	☐	☐	☐
House Type	☐	☐	☐
Exterior Siding	☐	☐	☐
Deck / Patio / Porch	☐	☐	☐
Garage	☐	☐	☐
Window / Doors	☐	☐	☐
Roof / Gutters	☐	☐	☐
Fencing	☐	☐	☐

HOME SYSTEMS

	Good	Average	Poor
Electrical	☐	☐	☐
Air Conditioning / Fans	☐	☐	☐
Heating	☐	☐	☐
Security	☐	☐	☐
Plumbing	☐	☐	☐
Intercom	☐	☐	☐

FEATURES

	Good	Average	Poor
Home Warranty	☐	☐	☐
Energy Saving Features	☐	☐	☐

INTERIOR

	Good	Average	Poor
Walls / Trim / Ceilings	☐	☐	☐
Flooring	☐	☐	☐
Stairs	☐	☐	☐
Storage	☐	☐	☐
Living Room	☐	☐	☐
Family Room	☐	☐	☐
Dining Room	☐	☐	☐

	Good	Average	Poor
Master Bedroom	☐	☐	☐
Bedroom 2	☐	☐	☐
Bedroom 3	☐	☐	☐
Bedroom 4	☐	☐	☐
Master Bathroom	☐	☐	☐
Bathroom 2	☐	☐	☐
Bathroom 3	☐	☐	☐
Bonus / Game Room	☐	☐	☐

	Good	Average	Poor
Kitchen	☐	☐	☐
Cabinets	☐	☐	☐
Countertop	☐	☐	☐
Counter Space	☐	☐	☐
Flooring	☐	☐	☐
Oven / Stove	☐	☐	☐
Microwave	☐	☐	☐
Layout	☐	☐	☐
Light Fixtures	☐	☐	☐
Backsplash	☐	☐	☐
Pantry	☐	☐	☐
Appliances	☐	☐	☐
Island	☐	☐	☐

	Good	Average	Poor
Basement	☐	☐	☐
Garage	☐	☐	☐

COMMUNITY

	Good	Average	Poor
Immediate Neighborhood	☐	☐	☐
Close to Employment	☐	☐	☐
Close to Shopping	☐	☐	☐
Close to Transportation	☐	☐	☐
Close to Schools / Daycare	☐	☐	☐
Close to Places of Worship	☐	☐	☐
Near Recreational Facilities	☐	☐	☐
Close to Airport	☐	☐	☐
Near Police and Fire Department	☐	☐	☐

Address ______________________________ Price ______________

Bedrooms __________ Bathrooms ___________ Sq.Ft. _______________

Lot Size: __________ Year Built ____________ School District _______

Annual Tax _________

EXTERIOR

	Good	Average	Poor
View/Yard/Landscaping	☐	☐	☐
Trees	☐	☐	☐
Lawn (Front)	☐	☐	☐
Lawn (Back)	☐	☐	☐
Fences (condition)	☐	☐	☐
Landscaping (condition)	☐	☐	☐
Irrigation / Sprinkler	☐	☐	☐
	☐	☐	☐
House Type	☐	☐	☐
Exterior Siding	☐	☐	☐
Deck / Patio / Porch	☐	☐	☐
Garage	☐	☐	☐
Window / Doors	☐	☐	☐
Roof / Gutters	☐	☐	☐
Fencing	☐	☐	☐

HOME SYSTEMS

	Good	Average	Poor
Electrical	☐	☐	☐
Air Conditioning / Fans	☐	☐	☐
Heating	☐	☐	☐
Security	☐	☐	☐
Plumbing	☐	☐	☐
Intercom	☐	☐	☐

FEATURES

	Good	Average	Poor
Home Warranty	☐	☐	☐
Energy Saving Features	☐	☐	☐

INTERIOR

	Good	Average	Poor
Walls / Trim / Ceilings	☐	☐	☐
Flooring	☐	☐	☐
Stairs	☐	☐	☐
Storage	☐	☐	☐
Living Room	☐	☐	☐
Family Room	☐	☐	☐
Dining Room	☐	☐	☐

	Good	Average	Poor
Master Bedroom	☐	☐	☐
Bedroom 2	☐	☐	☐
Bedroom 3	☐	☐	☐
Bedroom 4	☐	☐	☐
Master Bathroom	☐	☐	☐
Bathroom 2	☐	☐	☐
Bathroom 3	☐	☐	☐
Bonus / Game Room	☐	☐	☐

	Good	Average	Poor
Kitchen	☐	☐	☐
Cabinets	☐	☐	☐
Countertop	☐	☐	☐
Counter Space	☐	☐	☐
Flooring	☐	☐	☐
Oven / Stove	☐	☐	☐
Microwave	☐	☐	☐
Layout	☐	☐	☐
Light Fixtures	☐	☐	☐
Backsplash	☐	☐	☐
Pantry	☐	☐	☐
Appliances	☐	☐	☐
Island	☐	☐	☐

	Good	Average	Poor
Basement	☐	☐	☐
Garage	☐	☐	☐

COMMUNITY

	Good	Average	Poor
Immediate Neighborhood	☐	☐	☐
Close to Employment	☐	☐	☐
Close to Shopping	☐	☐	☐
Close to Transportation	☐	☐	☐
Close to Schools / Daycare	☐	☐	☐
Close to Places of Worship	☐	☐	☐
Near Recreational Facilities	☐	☐	☐
Close to Airport	☐	☐	☐
Near Police and Fire Department	☐	☐	☐

Address ____________________ Price ____________

Bedrooms ________ Bathrooms ________ Sq.Ft. ____________

Lot Size: ________ Year Built ________ School District ________

Annual Tax ________

EXTERIOR

	Good	Average	Poor
View/Yard/Landscaping	☐	☐	☐
Trees	☐	☐	☐
Lawn (Front)	☐	☐	☐
Lawn (Back)	☐	☐	☐
Fences (condition)	☐	☐	☐
Landscaping (condition)	☐	☐	☐
Irrigation / Sprinkler	☐	☐	☐
	☐	☐	☐
House Type	☐	☐	☐
Exterior Siding	☐	☐	☐
Deck / Patio / Porch	☐	☐	☐
Garage	☐	☐	☐
Window / Doors	☐	☐	☐
Roof / Gutters	☐	☐	☐
Fencing	☐	☐	☐

HOME SYSTEMS

	Good	Average	Poor
Electrical	☐	☐	☐
Air Conditioning / Fans	☐	☐	☐
Heating	☐	☐	☐
Security	☐	☐	☐
Plumbing	☐	☐	☐
Intercom	☐	☐	☐

FEATURES

	Good	Average	Poor
Home Warranty	☐	☐	☐
Energy Saving Features	☐	☐	☐

INTERIOR

	Good	Average	Poor
Walls / Trim / Ceilings	☐	☐	☐
Flooring	☐	☐	☐
Stairs	☐	☐	☐
Storage	☐	☐	☐
Living Room	☐	☐	☐
Family Room	☐	☐	☐
Dining Room	☐	☐	☐

	Good	Average	Poor
Master Bedroom	☐	☐	☐
Bedroom 2	☐	☐	☐
Bedroom 3	☐	☐	☐
Bedroom 4	☐	☐	☐
Master Bathroom	☐	☐	☐
Bathroom 2	☐	☐	☐
Bathroom 3	☐	☐	☐
Bonus / Game Room	☐	☐	☐

	Good	Average	Poor
Kitchen	☐	☐	☐
Cabinets	☐	☐	☐
Countertop	☐	☐	☐
Counter Space	☐	☐	☐
Flooring	☐	☐	☐
Oven / Stove	☐	☐	☐
Microwave	☐	☐	☐
Layout	☐	☐	☐
Light Fixtures	☐	☐	☐
Backsplash	☐	☐	☐
Pantry	☐	☐	☐
Appliances	☐	☐	☐
Island	☐	☐	☐

	Good	Average	Poor
Basement	☐	☐	☐
Garage	☐	☐	☐

COMMUNITY

	Good	Average	Poor
Immediate Neighborhood	☐	☐	☐
Close to Employment	☐	☐	☐
Close to Shopping	☐	☐	☐
Close to Transportation	☐	☐	☐
Close to Schools / Daycare	☐	☐	☐
Close to Places of Worship	☐	☐	☐
Near Recreational Facilities	☐	☐	☐
Close to Airport	☐	☐	☐
Near Police and Fire Department	☐	☐	☐

Address ______________________ Price ______________

Bedrooms ____________ Bathrooms ____________ Sq.Ft. ______________

Lot Size: ____________ Year Built ____________ School District ________

Annual Tax __________

EXTERIOR

	Good	Average	Poor
View/Yard/Landscaping	☐	☐	☐
Trees	☐	☐	☐
Lawn (Front)	☐	☐	☐
Lawn (Back)	☐	☐	☐
Fences (condition)	☐	☐	☐
Landscaping (condition)	☐	☐	☐
Irrigation / Sprinkler	☐	☐	☐
	☐	☐	☐
House Type	☐	☐	☐
Exterior Siding	☐	☐	☐
Deck / Patio / Porch	☐	☐	☐
Garage	☐	☐	☐
Window / Doors	☐	☐	☐
Roof / Gutters	☐	☐	☐
Fencing	☐	☐	☐

HOME SYSTEMS

	Good	Average	Poor
Electrical	☐	☐	☐
Air Conditioning / Fans	☐	☐	☐
Heating	☐	☐	☐
Security	☐	☐	☐
Plumbing	☐	☐	☐
Intercom	☐	☐	☐

FEATURES

	Good	Average	Poor
Home Warranty	☐	☐	☐
Energy Saving Features	☐	☐	☐

INTERIOR

	Good	Average	Poor
Walls / Trim / Ceilings	☐	☐	☐
Flooring	☐	☐	☐
Stairs	☐	☐	☐
Storage	☐	☐	☐
Living Room	☐	☐	☐
Family Room	☐	☐	☐
Dining Room	☐	☐	☐

	Good	Average	Poor
Master Bedroom	☐	☐	☐
Bedroom 2	☐	☐	☐
Bedroom 3	☐	☐	☐
Bedroom 4	☐	☐	☐
Master Bathroom	☐	☐	☐
Bathroom 2	☐	☐	☐
Bathroom 3	☐	☐	☐
Bonus / Game Room	☐	☐	☐

	Good	Average	Poor
Kitchen	☐	☐	☐
Cabinets	☐	☐	☐
Countertop	☐	☐	☐
Counter Space	☐	☐	☐
Flooring	☐	☐	☐
Oven / Stove	☐	☐	☐
Microwave	☐	☐	☐
Layout	☐	☐	☐
Light Fixtures	☐	☐	☐
Backsplash	☐	☐	☐
Pantry	☐	☐	☐
Appliances	☐	☐	☐
Island	☐	☐	☐

	Good	Average	Poor
Basement	☐	☐	☐
Garage	☐	☐	☐

COMMUNITY

	Good	Average	Poor
Immediate Neighborhood	☐	☐	☐
Close to Employment	☐	☐	☐
Close to Shopping	☐	☐	☐
Close to Transportation	☐	☐	☐
Close to Schools / Daycare	☐	☐	☐
Close to Places of Worship	☐	☐	☐
Near Recreational Facilities	☐	☐	☐
Close to Airport	☐	☐	☐
Near Police and Fire Department	☐	☐	☐

Address ______________________ Price ____________

Bedrooms ________ Bathrooms ________ Sq.Ft. ____________

Lot Size: ________ Year Built ________ School District ______

Annual Tax ________

EXTERIOR

	Good	Average	Poor
View/Yard/Landscaping	☐	☐	☐
Trees	☐	☐	☐
Lawn (Front)	☐	☐	☐
Lawn (Back)	☐	☐	☐
Fences (condition)	☐	☐	☐
Landscaping (condition)	☐	☐	☐
Irrigation / Sprinkler	☐	☐	☐
	☐	☐	☐
House Type	☐	☐	☐
Exterior Siding	☐	☐	☐
Deck / Patio / Porch	☐	☐	☐
Garage	☐	☐	☐
Window / Doors	☐	☐	☐
Roof / Gutters	☐	☐	☐
Fencing	☐	☐	☐

HOME SYSTEMS

	Good	Average	Poor
Electrical	☐	☐	☐
Air Conditioning / Fans	☐	☐	☐
Heating	☐	☐	☐
Security	☐	☐	☐
Plumbing	☐	☐	☐
Intercom	☐	☐	☐

FEATURES

	Good	Average	Poor
Home Warranty	☐	☐	☐
Energy Saving Features	☐	☐	☐

INTERIOR

	Good	Average	Poor
Walls / Trim / Ceilings	☐	☐	☐
Flooring	☐	☐	☐
Stairs	☐	☐	☐
Storage	☐	☐	☐
Living Room	☐	☐	☐
Family Room	☐	☐	☐
Dining Room	☐	☐	☐

	Good	Average	Poor
Master Bedroom	☐	☐	☐
Bedroom 2	☐	☐	☐
Bedroom 3	☐	☐	☐
Bedroom 4	☐	☐	☐
Master Bathroom	☐	☐	☐
Bathroom 2	☐	☐	☐
Bathroom 3	☐	☐	☐
Bonus / Game Room	☐	☐	☐

	Good	Average	Poor
Kitchen	☐	☐	☐
Cabinets	☐	☐	☐
Countertop	☐	☐	☐
Counter Space	☐	☐	☐
Flooring	☐	☐	☐
Oven / Stove	☐	☐	☐
Microwave	☐	☐	☐
Layout	☐	☐	☐
Light Fixtures	☐	☐	☐
Backsplash	☐	☐	☐
Pantry	☐	☐	☐
Appliances	☐	☐	☐
Island	☐	☐	☐

	Good	Average	Poor
Basement	☐	☐	☐
Garage	☐	☐	☐

COMMUNITY

	Good	Average	Poor
Immediate Neighborhood	☐	☐	☐
Close to Employment	☐	☐	☐
Close to Shopping	☐	☐	☐
Close to Transportation	☐	☐	☐
Close to Schools / Daycare	☐	☐	☐
Close to Places of Worship	☐	☐	☐
Near Recreational Facilities	☐	☐	☐
Close to Airport	☐	☐	☐
Near Police and Fire Department	☐	☐	☐

Address ______________________ Price __________

Bedrooms __________ Bathrooms __________ Sq.Ft. __________

Lot Size: __________ Year Built __________ School District ________

Annual Tax ________

EXTERIOR

	Good	Average	Poor
View/Yard/Landscaping	☐	☐	☐
Trees	☐	☐	☐
Lawn (Front)	☐	☐	☐
Lawn (Back)	☐	☐	☐
Fences (condition)	☐	☐	☐
Landscaping (condition)	☐	☐	☐
Irrigation / Sprinkler	☐	☐	☐
	☐	☐	☐
House Type	☐	☐	☐
Exterior Siding	☐	☐	☐
Deck / Patio / Porch	☐	☐	☐
Garage	☐	☐	☐
Window / Doors	☐	☐	☐
Roof / Gutters	☐	☐	☐
Fencing	☐	☐	☐

HOME SYSTEMS

	Good	Average	Poor
Electrical	☐	☐	☐
Air Conditioning / Fans	☐	☐	☐
Heating	☐	☐	☐
Security	☐	☐	☐
Plumbing	☐	☐	☐
Intercom	☐	☐	☐

FEATURES

	Good	Average	Poor
Home Warranty	☐	☐	☐
Energy Saving Features	☐	☐	☐

INTERIOR

	Good	Average	Poor
Walls / Trim / Ceilings	☐	☐	☐
Flooring	☐	☐	☐
Stairs	☐	☐	☐
Storage	☐	☐	☐
Living Room	☐	☐	☐
Family Room	☐	☐	☐
Dining Room	☐	☐	☐

	Good	Average	Poor
Master Bedroom	☐	☐	☐
Bedroom 2	☐	☐	☐
Bedroom 3	☐	☐	☐
Bedroom 4	☐	☐	☐
Master Bathroom	☐	☐	☐
Bathroom 2	☐	☐	☐
Bathroom 3	☐	☐	☐
Bonus / Game Room	☐	☐	☐

	Good	Average	Poor
Kitchen	☐	☐	☐
Cabinets	☐	☐	☐
Countertop	☐	☐	☐
Counter Space	☐	☐	☐
Flooring	☐	☐	☐
Oven / Stove	☐	☐	☐
Microwave	☐	☐	☐
Layout	☐	☐	☐
Light Fixtures	☐	☐	☐
Backsplash	☐	☐	☐
Pantry	☐	☐	☐
Appliances	☐	☐	☐
Island	☐	☐	☐

	Good	Average	Poor
Basement	☐	☐	☐
Garage	☐	☐	☐

COMMUNITY

	Good	Average	Poor
Immediate Neighborhood	☐	☐	☐
Close to Employment	☐	☐	☐
Close to Shopping	☐	☐	☐
Close to Transportation	☐	☐	☐
Close to Schools / Daycare	☐	☐	☐
Close to Places of Worship	☐	☐	☐
Near Recreational Facilities	☐	☐	☐
Close to Airport	☐	☐	☐
Near Police and Fire Department	☐	☐	☐

Address ______________________ Price ______________

Bedrooms __________ Bathrooms __________ Sq.Ft. ______________

Lot Size: __________ Year Built __________ School District __________

Annual Tax __________

EXTERIOR

	Good	Average	Poor
View/Yard/Landscaping	☐	☐	☐
Trees	☐	☐	☐
Lawn (Front)	☐	☐	☐
Lawn (Back)	☐	☐	☐
Fences (condition)	☐	☐	☐
Landscaping (condition)	☐	☐	☐
Irrigation / Sprinkler	☐	☐	☐
	☐	☐	☐
House Type	☐	☐	☐
Exterior Siding	☐	☐	☐
Deck / Patio / Porch	☐	☐	☐
Garage	☐	☐	☐
Window / Doors	☐	☐	☐
Roof / Gutters	☐	☐	☐
Fencing	☐	☐	☐

HOME SYSTEMS

	Good	Average	Poor
Electrical	☐	☐	☐
Air Conditioning / Fans	☐	☐	☐
Heating	☐	☐	☐
Security	☐	☐	☐
Plumbing	☐	☐	☐
Intercom	☐	☐	☐

FEATURES

	Good	Average	Poor
Home Warranty	☐	☐	☐
Energy Saving Features	☐	☐	☐

INTERIOR

	Good	Average	Poor
Walls / Trim / Ceilings	☐	☐	☐
Flooring	☐	☐	☐
Stairs	☐	☐	☐
Storage	☐	☐	☐
Living Room	☐	☐	☐
Family Room	☐	☐	☐
Dining Room	☐	☐	☐

	Good	Average	Poor
Master Bedroom	☐	☐	☐
Bedroom 2	☐	☐	☐
Bedroom 3	☐	☐	☐
Bedroom 4	☐	☐	☐
Master Bathroom	☐	☐	☐
Bathroom 2	☐	☐	☐
Bathroom 3	☐	☐	☐
Bonus / Game Room	☐	☐	☐

	Good	Average	Poor
Kitchen	☐	☐	☐
Cabinets	☐	☐	☐
Countertop	☐	☐	☐
Counter Space	☐	☐	☐
Flooring	☐	☐	☐
Oven / Stove	☐	☐	☐
Microwave	☐	☐	☐
Layout	☐	☐	☐
Light Fixtures	☐	☐	☐
Backsplash	☐	☐	☐
Pantry	☐	☐	☐
Appliances	☐	☐	☐
Island	☐	☐	☐

	Good	Average	Poor
Basement	☐	☐	☐
Garage	☐	☐	☐

COMMUNITY

	Good	Average	Poor
Immediate Neighborhood	☐	☐	☐
Close to Employment	☐	☐	☐
Close to Shopping	☐	☐	☐
Close to Transportation	☐	☐	☐
Close to Schools / Daycare	☐	☐	☐
Close to Places of Worship	☐	☐	☐
Near Recreational Facilities	☐	☐	☐
Close to Airport	☐	☐	☐
Near Police and Fire Department	☐	☐	☐

Address ______________________ Price ____________

Bedrooms ________ Bathrooms ________ Sq.Ft. ____________

Lot Size: ________ Year Built ________ School District ______

Annual Tax ________

EXTERIOR

	Good	Average	Poor
View/Yard/Landscaping	☐	☐	☐
Trees	☐	☐	☐
Lawn (Front)	☐	☐	☐
Lawn (Back)	☐	☐	☐
Fences (condition)	☐	☐	☐
Landscaping (condition)	☐	☐	☐
Irrigation / Sprinkler	☐	☐	☐
	☐	☐	☐
House Type	☐	☐	☐
Exterior Siding	☐	☐	☐
Deck / Patio / Porch	☐	☐	☐
Garage	☐	☐	☐
Window / Doors	☐	☐	☐
Roof / Gutters	☐	☐	☐
Fencing	☐	☐	☐

HOME SYSTEMS

	Good	Average	Poor
Electrical	☐	☐	☐
Air Conditioning / Fans	☐	☐	☐
Heating	☐	☐	☐
Security	☐	☐	☐
Plumbing	☐	☐	☐
Intercom	☐	☐	☐

FEATURES

	Good	Average	Poor
Home Warranty	☐	☐	☐
Energy Saving Features	☐	☐	☐

INTERIOR

	Good	Average	Poor
Walls / Trim / Ceilings	☐	☐	☐
Flooring	☐	☐	☐
Stairs	☐	☐	☐
Storage	☐	☐	☐
Living Room	☐	☐	☐
Family Room	☐	☐	☐
Dining Room	☐	☐	☐

	Good	Average	Poor
Master Bedroom	☐	☐	☐
Bedroom 2	☐	☐	☐
Bedroom 3	☐	☐	☐
Bedroom 4	☐	☐	☐
Master Bathroom	☐	☐	☐
Bathroom 2	☐	☐	☐
Bathroom 3	☐	☐	☐
Bonus / Game Room	☐	☐	☐

	Good	Average	Poor
Kitchen	☐	☐	☐
Cabinets	☐	☐	☐
Countertop	☐	☐	☐
Counter Space	☐	☐	☐
Flooring	☐	☐	☐
Oven / Stove	☐	☐	☐
Microwave	☐	☐	☐
Layout	☐	☐	☐
Light Fixtures	☐	☐	☐
Backsplash	☐	☐	☐
Pantry	☐	☐	☐
Appliances	☐	☐	☐
Island	☐	☐	☐

	Good	Average	Poor
Basement	☐	☐	☐
Garage	☐	☐	☐

COMMUNITY

	Good	Average	Poor
Immediate Neighborhood	☐	☐	☐
Close to Employment	☐	☐	☐
Close to Shopping	☐	☐	☐
Close to Transportation	☐	☐	☐
Close to Schools / Daycare	☐	☐	☐
Close to Places of Worship	☐	☐	☐
Near Recreational Facilities	☐	☐	☐
Close to Airport	☐	☐	☐
Near Police and Fire Department	☐	☐	☐

Address ____________________ Price ____________

Bedrooms ____________ Bathrooms ____________ Sq.Ft. ____________

Lot Size: ____________ Year Built ____________ School District ____________

Annual Tax ____________

EXTERIOR

	Good	Average	Poor
View/Yard/Landscaping	☐	☐	☐
Trees	☐	☐	☐
Lawn (Front)	☐	☐	☐
Lawn (Back)	☐	☐	☐
Fences (condition)	☐	☐	☐
Landscaping (condition)	☐	☐	☐
Irrigation / Sprinkler	☐	☐	☐
	☐	☐	☐
House Type	☐	☐	☐
Exterior Siding	☐	☐	☐
Deck / Patio / Porch	☐	☐	☐
Garage	☐	☐	☐
Window / Doors	☐	☐	☐
Roof / Gutters	☐	☐	☐
Fencing	☐	☐	☐

HOME SYSTEMS

	Good	Average	Poor
Electrical	☐	☐	☐
Air Conditioning / Fans	☐	☐	☐
Heating	☐	☐	☐
Security	☐	☐	☐
Plumbing	☐	☐	☐
Intercom	☐	☐	☐

FEATURES

	Good	Average	Poor
Home Warranty	☐	☐	☐
Energy Saving Features	☐	☐	☐

INTERIOR

	Good	Average	Poor
Walls / Trim / Ceilings	☐	☐	☐
Flooring	☐	☐	☐
Stairs	☐	☐	☐
Storage	☐	☐	☐
Living Room	☐	☐	☐
Family Room	☐	☐	☐
Dining Room	☐	☐	☐

	Good	Average	Poor
Master Bedroom	☐	☐	☐
Bedroom 2	☐	☐	☐
Bedroom 3	☐	☐	☐
Bedroom 4	☐	☐	☐
Master Bathroom	☐	☐	☐
Bathroom 2	☐	☐	☐
Bathroom 3	☐	☐	☐
Bonus / Game Room	☐	☐	☐

	Good	Average	Poor
Kitchen	☐	☐	☐
Cabinets	☐	☐	☐
Countertop	☐	☐	☐
Counter Space	☐	☐	☐
Flooring	☐	☐	☐
Oven / Stove	☐	☐	☐
Microwave	☐	☐	☐
Layout	☐	☐	☐
Light Fixtures	☐	☐	☐
Backsplash	☐	☐	☐
Pantry	☐	☐	☐
Appliances	☐	☐	☐
Island	☐	☐	☐

	Good	Average	Poor
Basement	☐	☐	☐
Garage	☐	☐	☐

COMMUNITY

	Good	Average	Poor
Immediate Neighborhood	☐	☐	☐
Close to Employment	☐	☐	☐
Close to Shopping	☐	☐	☐
Close to Transportation	☐	☐	☐
Close to Schools / Daycare	☐	☐	☐
Close to Places of Worship	☐	☐	☐
Near Recreational Facilities	☐	☐	☐
Close to Airport	☐	☐	☐
Near Police and Fire Department	☐	☐	☐

Address ____________________ Price ____________

Bedrooms ________ Bathrooms ________ Sq.Ft. ____________

Lot Size: ________ Year Built ________ School District ________

Annual Tax ________

EXTERIOR

	Good	Average	Poor
View/Yard/Landscaping	☐	☐	☐
Trees	☐	☐	☐
Lawn (Front)	☐	☐	☐
Lawn (Back)	☐	☐	☐
Fences (condition)	☐	☐	☐
Landscaping (condition)	☐	☐	☐
Irrigation / Sprinkler	☐	☐	☐
	☐	☐	☐
House Type	☐	☐	☐
Exterior Siding	☐	☐	☐
Deck / Patio / Porch	☐	☐	☐
Garage	☐	☐	☐
Window / Doors	☐	☐	☐
Roof / Gutters	☐	☐	☐
Fencing	☐	☐	☐

HOME SYSTEMS

	Good	Average	Poor
Electrical	☐	☐	☐
Air Conditioning / Fans	☐	☐	☐
Heating	☐	☐	☐
Security	☐	☐	☐
Plumbing	☐	☐	☐
Intercom	☐	☐	☐

FEATURES

	Good	Average	Poor
Home Warranty	☐	☐	☐
Energy Saving Features	☐	☐	☐

INTERIOR

	Good	Average	Poor
Walls / Trim / Ceilings	☐	☐	☐
Flooring	☐	☐	☐
Stairs	☐	☐	☐
Storage	☐	☐	☐
Living Room	☐	☐	☐
Family Room	☐	☐	☐
Dining Room	☐	☐	☐

	Good	Average	Poor
Master Bedroom	☐	☐	☐
Bedroom 2	☐	☐	☐
Bedroom 3	☐	☐	☐
Bedroom 4	☐	☐	☐
Master Bathroom	☐	☐	☐
Bathroom 2	☐	☐	☐
Bathroom 3	☐	☐	☐
Bonus / Game Room	☐	☐	☐

	Good	Average	Poor
Kitchen	☐	☐	☐
Cabinets	☐	☐	☐
Countertop	☐	☐	☐
Counter Space	☐	☐	☐
Flooring	☐	☐	☐
Oven / Stove	☐	☐	☐
Microwave	☐	☐	☐
Layout	☐	☐	☐
Light Fixtures	☐	☐	☐
Backsplash	☐	☐	☐
Pantry	☐	☐	☐
Appliances	☐	☐	☐
Island	☐	☐	☐

	Good	Average	Poor
Basement	☐	☐	☐
Garage	☐	☐	☐

COMMUNITY

	Good	Average	Poor
Immediate Neighborhood	☐	☐	☐
Close to Employment	☐	☐	☐
Close to Shopping	☐	☐	☐
Close to Transportation	☐	☐	☐
Close to Schools / Daycare	☐	☐	☐
Close to Places of Worship	☐	☐	☐
Near Recreational Facilities	☐	☐	☐
Close to Airport	☐	☐	☐
Near Police and Fire Department	☐	☐	☐

Address ______________________ Price ______________

Bedrooms ____________ Bathrooms ____________ Sq.Ft. ______________

Lot Size: ____________ Year Built ____________ School District ________

Annual Tax ____________

EXTERIOR

	Good	Average	Poor
View/Yard/Landscaping	☐	☐	☐
Trees	☐	☐	☐
Lawn (Front)	☐	☐	☐
Lawn (Back)	☐	☐	☐
Fences (condition)	☐	☐	☐
Landscaping (condition)	☐	☐	☐
Irrigation / Sprinkler	☐	☐	☐
	☐	☐	☐
House Type	☐	☐	☐
Exterior Siding	☐	☐	☐
Deck / Patio / Porch	☐	☐	☐
Garage	☐	☐	☐
Window / Doors	☐	☐	☐
Roof / Gutters	☐	☐	☐
Fencing	☐	☐	☐

HOME SYSTEMS

	Good	Average	Poor
Electrical	☐	☐	☐
Air Conditioning / Fans	☐	☐	☐
Heating	☐	☐	☐
Security	☐	☐	☐
Plumbing	☐	☐	☐
Intercom	☐	☐	☐

FEATURES

	Good	Average	Poor
Home Warranty	☐	☐	☐
Energy Saving Features	☐	☐	☐

INTERIOR

	Good	Average	Poor
Walls / Trim / Ceilings	☐	☐	☐
Flooring	☐	☐	☐
Stairs	☐	☐	☐
Storage	☐	☐	☐
Living Room	☐	☐	☐
Family Room	☐	☐	☐
Dining Room	☐	☐	☐

	Good	Average	Poor
Master Bedroom	☐	☐	☐
Bedroom 2	☐	☐	☐
Bedroom 3	☐	☐	☐
Bedroom 4	☐	☐	☐
Master Bathroom	☐	☐	☐
Bathroom 2	☐	☐	☐
Bathroom 3	☐	☐	☐
Bonus / Game Room	☐	☐	☐

	Good	Average	Poor
Kitchen	☐	☐	☐
Cabinets	☐	☐	☐
Countertop	☐	☐	☐
Counter Space	☐	☐	☐
Flooring	☐	☐	☐
Oven / Stove	☐	☐	☐
Microwave	☐	☐	☐
Layout	☐	☐	☐
Light Fixtures	☐	☐	☐
Backsplash	☐	☐	☐
Pantry	☐	☐	☐
Appliances	☐	☐	☐
Island	☐	☐	☐

	Good	Average	Poor
Basement	☐	☐	☐
Garage	☐	☐	☐

COMMUNITY

	Good	Average	Poor
Immediate Neighborhood	☐	☐	☐
Close to Employment	☐	☐	☐
Close to Shopping	☐	☐	☐
Close to Transportation	☐	☐	☐
Close to Schools / Daycare	☐	☐	☐
Close to Places of Worship	☐	☐	☐
Near Recreational Facilities	☐	☐	☐
Close to Airport	☐	☐	☐
Near Police and Fire Department	☐	☐	☐

Address ________________________ Price ____________

Bedrooms ____________ Bathrooms ____________ Sq.Ft. ____________

Lot Size: ____________ Year Built ____________ School District ____________

Annual Tax ____________

EXTERIOR

	Good	Average	Poor
View/Yard/Landscaping	☐	☐	☐
Trees	☐	☐	☐
Lawn (Front)	☐	☐	☐
Lawn (Back)	☐	☐	☐
Fences (condition)	☐	☐	☐
Landscaping (condition)	☐	☐	☐
Irrigation / Sprinkler	☐	☐	☐
	☐	☐	☐
House Type	☐	☐	☐
Exterior Siding	☐	☐	☐
Deck / Patio / Porch	☐	☐	☐
Garage	☐	☐	☐
Window / Doors	☐	☐	☐
Roof / Gutters	☐	☐	☐
Fencing	☐	☐	☐

HOME SYSTEMS

	Good	Average	Poor
Electrical	☐	☐	☐
Air Conditioning / Fans	☐	☐	☐
Heating	☐	☐	☐
Security	☐	☐	☐
Plumbing	☐	☐	☐
Intercom	☐	☐	☐

FEATURES

	Good	Average	Poor
Home Warranty	☐	☐	☐
Energy Saving Features	☐	☐	☐

INTERIOR

	Good	Average	Poor
Walls / Trim / Ceilings	☐	☐	☐
Flooring	☐	☐	☐
Stairs	☐	☐	☐
Storage	☐	☐	☐
Living Room	☐	☐	☐
Family Room	☐	☐	☐
Dining Room	☐	☐	☐

	Good	Average	Poor
Master Bedroom	☐	☐	☐
Bedroom 2	☐	☐	☐
Bedroom 3	☐	☐	☐
Bedroom 4	☐	☐	☐
Master Bathroom	☐	☐	☐
Bathroom 2	☐	☐	☐
Bathroom 3	☐	☐	☐
Bonus / Game Room	☐	☐	☐

	Good	Average	Poor
Kitchen	☐	☐	☐
Cabinets	☐	☐	☐
Countertop	☐	☐	☐
Counter Space	☐	☐	☐
Flooring	☐	☐	☐
Oven / Stove	☐	☐	☐
Microwave	☐	☐	☐
Layout	☐	☐	☐
Light Fixtures	☐	☐	☐
Backsplash	☐	☐	☐
Pantry	☐	☐	☐
Appliances	☐	☐	☐
Island	☐	☐	☐

	Good	Average	Poor
Basement	☐	☐	☐
Garage	☐	☐	☐

COMMUNITY

	Good	Average	Poor
Immediate Neighborhood	☐	☐	☐
Close to Employment	☐	☐	☐
Close to Shopping	☐	☐	☐
Close to Transportation	☐	☐	☐
Close to Schools / Daycare	☐	☐	☐
Close to Places of Worship	☐	☐	☐
Near Recreational Facilities	☐	☐	☐
Close to Airport	☐	☐	☐
Near Police and Fire Department	☐	☐	☐

Address ______________________ Price ______________

Bedrooms __________ Bathrooms __________ Sq.Ft. ______________

Lot Size: __________ Year Built __________ School District ______

Annual Tax __________

EXTERIOR

	Good	Average	Poor
View/Yard/Landscaping	☐	☐	☐
Trees	☐	☐	☐
Lawn (Front)	☐	☐	☐
Lawn (Back)	☐	☐	☐
Fences (condition)	☐	☐	☐
Landscaping (condition)	☐	☐	☐
Irrigation / Sprinkler	☐	☐	☐
	☐	☐	☐
House Type	☐	☐	☐
Exterior Siding	☐	☐	☐
Deck / Patio / Porch	☐	☐	☐
Garage	☐	☐	☐
Window / Doors	☐	☐	☐
Roof / Gutters	☐	☐	☐
Fencing	☐	☐	☐

HOME SYSTEMS

	Good	Average	Poor
Electrical	☐	☐	☐
Air Conditioning / Fans	☐	☐	☐
Heating	☐	☐	☐
Security	☐	☐	☐
Plumbing	☐	☐	☐
Intercom	☐	☐	☐

FEATURES

	Good	Average	Poor
Home Warranty	☐	☐	☐
Energy Saving Features	☐	☐	☐

INTERIOR

	Good	Average	Poor
Walls / Trim / Ceilings	☐	☐	☐
Flooring	☐	☐	☐
Stairs	☐	☐	☐
Storage	☐	☐	☐
Living Room	☐	☐	☐
Family Room	☐	☐	☐
Dining Room	☐	☐	☐

	Good	Average	Poor
Master Bedroom	☐	☐	☐
Bedroom 2	☐	☐	☐
Bedroom 3	☐	☐	☐
Bedroom 4	☐	☐	☐
Master Bathroom	☐	☐	☐
Bathroom 2	☐	☐	☐
Bathroom 3	☐	☐	☐
Bonus / Game Room	☐	☐	☐

	Good	Average	Poor
Kitchen	☐	☐	☐
Cabinets	☐	☐	☐
Countertop	☐	☐	☐
Counter Space	☐	☐	☐
Flooring	☐	☐	☐
Oven / Stove	☐	☐	☐
Microwave	☐	☐	☐
Layout	☐	☐	☐
Light Fixtures	☐	☐	☐
Backsplash	☐	☐	☐
Pantry	☐	☐	☐
Appliances	☐	☐	☐
Island	☐	☐	☐

	Good	Average	Poor
Basement	☐	☐	☐
Garage	☐	☐	☐

COMMUNITY

	Good	Average	Poor
Immediate Neighborhood	☐	☐	☐
Close to Employment	☐	☐	☐
Close to Shopping	☐	☐	☐
Close to Transportation	☐	☐	☐
Close to Schools / Daycare	☐	☐	☐
Close to Places of Worship	☐	☐	☐
Near Recreational Facilities	☐	☐	☐
Close to Airport	☐	☐	☐
Near Police and Fire Department	☐	☐	☐

Address ______________________ Price ______________

Bedrooms ___________ Bathrooms ___________ Sq.Ft. ______________

Lot Size: ___________ Year Built ___________ School District ________

Annual Tax ___________

EXTERIOR

	Good	Average	Poor
View/Yard/Landscaping	☐	☐	☐
Trees	☐	☐	☐
Lawn (Front)	☐	☐	☐
Lawn (Back)	☐	☐	☐
Fences (condition)	☐	☐	☐
Landscaping (condition)	☐	☐	☐
Irrigation / Sprinkler	☐	☐	☐
	☐	☐	☐
House Type	☐	☐	☐
Exterior Siding	☐	☐	☐
Deck / Patio / Porch	☐	☐	☐
Garage	☐	☐	☐
Window / Doors	☐	☐	☐
Roof / Gutters	☐	☐	☐
Fencing	☐	☐	☐

HOME SYSTEMS

	Good	Average	Poor
Electrical	☐	☐	☐
Air Conditioning / Fans	☐	☐	☐
Heating	☐	☐	☐
Security	☐	☐	☐
Plumbing	☐	☐	☐
Intercom	☐	☐	☐

FEATURES

	Good	Average	Poor
Home Warranty	☐	☐	☐
Energy Saving Features	☐	☐	☐

INTERIOR

	Good	Average	Poor
Walls / Trim / Ceilings	☐	☐	☐
Flooring	☐	☐	☐
Stairs	☐	☐	☐
Storage	☐	☐	☐
Living Room	☐	☐	☐
Family Room	☐	☐	☐
Dining Room	☐	☐	☐

	Good	Average	Poor
Master Bedroom	☐	☐	☐
Bedroom 2	☐	☐	☐
Bedroom 3	☐	☐	☐
Bedroom 4	☐	☐	☐
Master Bathroom	☐	☐	☐
Bathroom 2	☐	☐	☐
Bathroom 3	☐	☐	☐
Bonus / Game Room	☐	☐	☐

	Good	Average	Poor
Kitchen	☐	☐	☐
Cabinets	☐	☐	☐
Countertop	☐	☐	☐
Counter Space	☐	☐	☐
Flooring	☐	☐	☐
Oven / Stove	☐	☐	☐
Microwave	☐	☐	☐
Layout	☐	☐	☐
Light Fixtures	☐	☐	☐
Backsplash	☐	☐	☐
Pantry	☐	☐	☐
Appliances	☐	☐	☐
Island	☐	☐	☐

	Good	Average	Poor
Basement	☐	☐	☐
Garage	☐	☐	☐

COMMUNITY

	Good	Average	Poor
Immediate Neighborhood	☐	☐	☐
Close to Employment	☐	☐	☐
Close to Shopping	☐	☐	☐
Close to Transportation	☐	☐	☐
Close to Schools / Daycare	☐	☐	☐
Close to Places of Worship	☐	☐	☐
Near Recreational Facilities	☐	☐	☐
Close to Airport	☐	☐	☐
Near Police and Fire Department	☐	☐	☐

Address ______________________________ Price ______________

Bedrooms __________ Bathrooms __________ Sq.Ft. ______________

Lot Size: __________ Year Built ____________ School District _______

Annual Tax _________

EXTERIOR

	Good	Average	Poor
View/Yard/Landscaping	☐	☐	☐
Trees	☐	☐	☐
Lawn (Front)	☐	☐	☐
Lawn (Back)	☐	☐	☐
Fences (condition)	☐	☐	☐
Landscaping (condition)	☐	☐	☐
Irrigation / Sprinkler	☐	☐	☐
	☐	☐	☐
House Type	☐	☐	☐
Exterior Siding	☐	☐	☐
Deck / Patio / Porch	☐	☐	☐
Garage	☐	☐	☐
Window / Doors	☐	☐	☐
Roof / Gutters	☐	☐	☐
Fencing	☐	☐	☐

HOME SYSTEMS

	Good	Average	Poor
Electrical	☐	☐	☐
Air Conditioning / Fans	☐	☐	☐
Heating	☐	☐	☐
Security	☐	☐	☐
Plumbing	☐	☐	☐
Intercom	☐	☐	☐

FEATURES

	Good	Average	Poor
Home Warranty	☐	☐	☐
Energy Saving Features	☐	☐	☐

INTERIOR

	Good	Average	Poor
Walls / Trim / Ceilings	☐	☐	☐
Flooring	☐	☐	☐
Stairs	☐	☐	☐
Storage	☐	☐	☐
Living Room	☐	☐	☐
Family Room	☐	☐	☐
Dining Room	☐	☐	☐

	Good	Average	Poor
Master Bedroom	☐	☐	☐
Bedroom 2	☐	☐	☐
Bedroom 3	☐	☐	☐
Bedroom 4	☐	☐	☐
Master Bathroom	☐	☐	☐
Bathroom 2	☐	☐	☐
Bathroom 3	☐	☐	☐
Bonus / Game Room	☐	☐	☐

	Good	Average	Poor
Kitchen	☐	☐	☐
Cabinets	☐	☐	☐
Countertop	☐	☐	☐
Counter Space	☐	☐	☐
Flooring	☐	☐	☐
Oven / Stove	☐	☐	☐
Microwave	☐	☐	☐
Layout	☐	☐	☐
Light Fixtures	☐	☐	☐
Backsplash	☐	☐	☐
Pantry	☐	☐	☐
Appliances	☐	☐	☐
Island	☐	☐	☐

	Good	Average	Poor
Basement	☐	☐	☐
Garage	☐	☐	☐

COMMUNITY

	Good	Average	Poor
Immediate Neighborhood	☐	☐	☐
Close to Employment	☐	☐	☐
Close to Shopping	☐	☐	☐
Close to Transportation	☐	☐	☐
Close to Schools / Daycare	☐	☐	☐
Close to Places of Worship	☐	☐	☐
Near Recreational Facilities	☐	☐	☐
Close to Airport	☐	☐	☐
Near Police and Fire Department	☐	☐	☐

Address ______________________ Price ____________

Bedrooms ________ Bathrooms ________ Sq.Ft. ____________

Lot Size: ________ Year Built ________ School District ________

Annual Tax ________

EXTERIOR

	Good	Average	Poor
View/Yard/Landscaping	☐	☐	☐
Trees	☐	☐	☐
Lawn (Front)	☐	☐	☐
Lawn (Back)	☐	☐	☐
Fences (condition)	☐	☐	☐
Landscaping (condition)	☐	☐	☐
Irrigation / Sprinkler	☐	☐	☐
	☐	☐	☐
House Type	☐	☐	☐
Exterior Siding	☐	☐	☐
Deck / Patio / Porch	☐	☐	☐
Garage	☐	☐	☐
Window / Doors	☐	☐	☐
Roof / Gutters	☐	☐	☐
Fencing	☐	☐	☐

HOME SYSTEMS

	Good	Average	Poor
Electrical	☐	☐	☐
Air Conditioning / Fans	☐	☐	☐
Heating	☐	☐	☐
Security	☐	☐	☐
Plumbing	☐	☐	☐
Intercom	☐	☐	☐

FEATURES

	Good	Average	Poor
Home Warranty	☐	☐	☐
Energy Saving Features	☐	☐	☐

INTERIOR

	Good	Average	Poor
Walls / Trim / Ceilings	☐	☐	☐
Flooring	☐	☐	☐
Stairs	☐	☐	☐
Storage	☐	☐	☐
Living Room	☐	☐	☐
Family Room	☐	☐	☐
Dining Room	☐	☐	☐

	Good	Average	Poor
Master Bedroom	☐	☐	☐
Bedroom 2	☐	☐	☐
Bedroom 3	☐	☐	☐
Bedroom 4	☐	☐	☐
Master Bathroom	☐	☐	☐
Bathroom 2	☐	☐	☐
Bathroom 3	☐	☐	☐
Bonus / Game Room	☐	☐	☐

Kitchen	Good	Average	Poor
	☐	☐	☐
Cabinets	☐	☐	☐
Countertop	☐	☐	☐
Counter Space	☐	☐	☐
Flooring	☐	☐	☐
Oven / Stove	☐	☐	☐
Microwave	☐	☐	☐
Layout	☐	☐	☐
Light Fixtures	☐	☐	☐
Backsplash	☐	☐	☐
Pantry	☐	☐	☐
Appliances	☐	☐	☐
Island	☐	☐	☐

	Good	Average	Poor
Basement	☐	☐	☐
Garage	☐	☐	☐

COMMUNITY

	Good	Average	Poor
Immediate Neighborhood	☐	☐	☐
Close to Employment	☐	☐	☐
Close to Shopping	☐	☐	☐
Close to Transportation	☐	☐	☐
Close to Schools / Daycare	☐	☐	☐
Close to Places of Worship	☐	☐	☐
Near Recreational Facilities	☐	☐	☐
Close to Airport	☐	☐	☐
Near Police and Fire Department	☐	☐	☐

Address ____________________ Price ____________

Bedrooms ________ Bathrooms ________ Sq.Ft. ____________

Lot Size: ________ Year Built ________ School District ______

Annual Tax ________

EXTERIOR

	Good	Average	Poor
View/Yard/Landscaping	☐	☐	☐
Trees	☐	☐	☐
Lawn (Front)	☐	☐	☐
Lawn (Back)	☐	☐	☐
Fences (condition)	☐	☐	☐
Landscaping (condition)	☐	☐	☐
Irrigation / Sprinkler	☐	☐	☐
	☐	☐	☐
House Type	☐	☐	☐
Exterior Siding	☐	☐	☐
Deck / Patio / Porch	☐	☐	☐
Garage	☐	☐	☐
Window / Doors	☐	☐	☐
Roof / Gutters	☐	☐	☐
Fencing	☐	☐	☐

HOME SYSTEMS

	Good	Average	Poor
Electrical	☐	☐	☐
Air Conditioning / Fans	☐	☐	☐
Heating	☐	☐	☐
Security	☐	☐	☐
Plumbing	☐	☐	☐
Intercom	☐	☐	☐

FEATURES

	Good	Average	Poor
Home Warranty	☐	☐	☐
Energy Saving Features	☐	☐	☐

INTERIOR

	Good	Average	Poor
Walls / Trim / Ceilings	☐	☐	☐
Flooring	☐	☐	☐
Stairs	☐	☐	☐
Storage	☐	☐	☐
Living Room	☐	☐	☐
Family Room	☐	☐	☐
Dining Room	☐	☐	☐

	Good	Average	Poor
Master Bedroom	☐	☐	☐
Bedroom 2	☐	☐	☐
Bedroom 3	☐	☐	☐
Bedroom 4	☐	☐	☐
Master Bathroom	☐	☐	☐
Bathroom 2	☐	☐	☐
Bathroom 3	☐	☐	☐
Bonus / Game Room	☐	☐	☐

	Good	Average	Poor
Kitchen	☐	☐	☐
Cabinets	☐	☐	☐
Countertop	☐	☐	☐
Counter Space	☐	☐	☐
Flooring	☐	☐	☐
Oven / Stove	☐	☐	☐
Microwave	☐	☐	☐
Layout	☐	☐	☐
Light Fixtures	☐	☐	☐
Backsplash	☐	☐	☐
Pantry	☐	☐	☐
Appliances	☐	☐	☐
Island	☐	☐	☐

	Good	Average	Poor
Basement	☐	☐	☐
Garage	☐	☐	☐

COMMUNITY

	Good	Average	Poor
Immediate Neighborhood	☐	☐	☐
Close to Employment	☐	☐	☐
Close to Shopping	☐	☐	☐
Close to Transportation	☐	☐	☐
Close to Schools / Daycare	☐	☐	☐
Close to Places of Worship	☐	☐	☐
Near Recreational Facilities	☐	☐	☐
Close to Airport	☐	☐	☐
Near Police and Fire Department	☐	☐	☐

Address ______________________ Price ______________

Bedrooms __________ Bathrooms __________ Sq.Ft. ______________

Lot Size: __________ Year Built __________ School District ________

Annual Tax __________

EXTERIOR

	Good	Average	Poor
View/Yard/Landscaping	☐	☐	☐
Trees	☐	☐	☐
Lawn (Front)	☐	☐	☐
Lawn (Back)	☐	☐	☐
Fences (condition)	☐	☐	☐
Landscaping (condition)	☐	☐	☐
Irrigation / Sprinkler	☐	☐	☐
	☐	☐	☐
House Type	☐	☐	☐
Exterior Siding	☐	☐	☐
Deck / Patio / Porch	☐	☐	☐
Garage	☐	☐	☐
Window / Doors	☐	☐	☐
Roof / Gutters	☐	☐	☐
Fencing	☐	☐	☐

HOME SYSTEMS

	Good	Average	Poor
Electrical	☐	☐	☐
Air Conditioning / Fans	☐	☐	☐
Heating	☐	☐	☐
Security	☐	☐	☐
Plumbing	☐	☐	☐
Intercom	☐	☐	☐

FEATURES

	Good	Average	Poor
Home Warranty	☐	☐	☐
Energy Saving Features	☐	☐	☐

INTERIOR

	Good	Average	Poor
Walls / Trim / Ceilings	☐	☐	☐
Flooring	☐	☐	☐
Stairs	☐	☐	☐
Storage	☐	☐	☐
Living Room	☐	☐	☐
Family Room	☐	☐	☐
Dining Room	☐	☐	☐

	Good	Average	Poor
Master Bedroom	☐	☐	☐
Bedroom 2	☐	☐	☐
Bedroom 3	☐	☐	☐
Bedroom 4	☐	☐	☐
Master Bathroom	☐	☐	☐
Bathroom 2	☐	☐	☐
Bathroom 3	☐	☐	☐
Bonus / Game Room	☐	☐	☐

	Good	Average	Poor
Kitchen	☐	☐	☐
Cabinets	☐	☐	☐
Countertop	☐	☐	☐
Counter Space	☐	☐	☐
Flooring	☐	☐	☐
Oven / Stove	☐	☐	☐
Microwave	☐	☐	☐
Layout	☐	☐	☐
Light Fixtures	☐	☐	☐
Backsplash	☐	☐	☐
Pantry	☐	☐	☐
Appliances	☐	☐	☐
Island	☐	☐	☐

	Good	Average	Poor
Basement	☐	☐	☐
Garage	☐	☐	☐

COMMUNITY

	Good	Average	Poor
Immediate Neighborhood	☐	☐	☐
Close to Employment	☐	☐	☐
Close to Shopping	☐	☐	☐
Close to Transportation	☐	☐	☐
Close to Schools / Daycare	☐	☐	☐
Close to Places of Worship	☐	☐	☐
Near Recreational Facilities	☐	☐	☐
Close to Airport	☐	☐	☐
Near Police and Fire Department	☐	☐	☐

Address ____________________ Price ____________

Bedrooms ________ Bathrooms ________ Sq.Ft. ____________

Lot Size: ________ Year Built ________ School District ________

Annual Tax ________

EXTERIOR

	Good	Average	Poor
View/Yard/Landscaping	☐	☐	☐
Trees	☐	☐	☐
Lawn (Front)	☐	☐	☐
Lawn (Back)	☐	☐	☐
Fences (condition)	☐	☐	☐
Landscaping (condition)	☐	☐	☐
Irrigation / Sprinkler	☐	☐	☐
	☐	☐	☐
House Type	☐	☐	☐
Exterior Siding	☐	☐	☐
Deck / Patio / Porch	☐	☐	☐
Garage	☐	☐	☐
Window / Doors	☐	☐	☐
Roof / Gutters	☐	☐	☐
Fencing	☐	☐	☐

HOME SYSTEMS

	Good	Average	Poor
Electrical	☐	☐	☐
Air Conditioning / Fans	☐	☐	☐
Heating	☐	☐	☐
Security	☐	☐	☐
Plumbing	☐	☐	☐
Intercom	☐	☐	☐

FEATURES

	Good	Average	Poor
Home Warranty	☐	☐	☐
Energy Saving Features	☐	☐	☐

INTERIOR

	Good	Average	Poor
Walls / Trim / Ceilings	☐	☐	☐
Flooring	☐	☐	☐
Stairs	☐	☐	☐
Storage	☐	☐	☐
Living Room	☐	☐	☐
Family Room	☐	☐	☐
Dining Room	☐	☐	☐

	Good	Average	Poor
Master Bedroom	☐	☐	☐
Bedroom 2	☐	☐	☐
Bedroom 3	☐	☐	☐
Bedroom 4	☐	☐	☐
Master Bathroom	☐	☐	☐
Bathroom 2	☐	☐	☐
Bathroom 3	☐	☐	☐
Bonus / Game Room	☐	☐	☐

	Good	Average	Poor
Kitchen	☐	☐	☐
Cabinets	☐	☐	☐
Countertop	☐	☐	☐
Counter Space	☐	☐	☐
Flooring	☐	☐	☐
Oven / Stove	☐	☐	☐
Microwave	☐	☐	☐
Layout	☐	☐	☐
Light Fixtures	☐	☐	☐
Backsplash	☐	☐	☐
Pantry	☐	☐	☐
Appliances	☐	☐	☐
Island	☐	☐	☐

	Good	Average	Poor
Basement	☐	☐	☐
Garage	☐	☐	☐

COMMUNITY

	Good	Average	Poor
Immediate Neighborhood	☐	☐	☐
Close to Employment	☐	☐	☐
Close to Shopping	☐	☐	☐
Close to Transportation	☐	☐	☐
Close to Schools / Daycare	☐	☐	☐
Close to Places of Worship	☐	☐	☐
Near Recreational Facilities	☐	☐	☐
Close to Airport	☐	☐	☐
Near Police and Fire Department	☐	☐	☐

Address ____________________ Price ____________

Bedrooms ________ Bathrooms ________ Sq.Ft. ____________

Lot Size: ________ Year Built ________ School District ________

Annual Tax ________

EXTERIOR

	Good	Average	Poor
View/Yard/Landscaping	☐	☐	☐
Trees	☐	☐	☐
Lawn (Front)	☐	☐	☐
Lawn (Back)	☐	☐	☐
Fences (condition)	☐	☐	☐
Landscaping (condition)	☐	☐	☐
Irrigation / Sprinkler	☐	☐	☐
	☐	☐	☐
House Type	☐	☐	☐
Exterior Siding	☐	☐	☐
Deck / Patio / Porch	☐	☐	☐
Garage	☐	☐	☐
Window / Doors	☐	☐	☐
Roof / Gutters	☐	☐	☐
Fencing	☐	☐	☐

HOME SYSTEMS

	Good	Average	Poor
Electrical	☐	☐	☐
Air Conditioning / Fans	☐	☐	☐
Heating	☐	☐	☐
Security	☐	☐	☐
Plumbing	☐	☐	☐
Intercom	☐	☐	☐

FEATURES

	Good	Average	Poor
Home Warranty	☐	☐	☐
Energy Saving Features	☐	☐	☐

INTERIOR

	Good	Average	Poor
Walls / Trim / Ceilings	☐	☐	☐
Flooring	☐	☐	☐
Stairs	☐	☐	☐
Storage	☐	☐	☐
Living Room	☐	☐	☐
Family Room	☐	☐	☐
Dining Room	☐	☐	☐

	Good	Average	Poor
Master Bedroom	☐	☐	☐
Bedroom 2	☐	☐	☐
Bedroom 3	☐	☐	☐
Bedroom 4	☐	☐	☐
Master Bathroom	☐	☐	☐
Bathroom 2	☐	☐	☐
Bathroom 3	☐	☐	☐
Bonus / Game Room	☐	☐	☐

	Good	Average	Poor
Kitchen	☐	☐	☐
Cabinets	☐	☐	☐
Countertop	☐	☐	☐
Counter Space	☐	☐	☐
Flooring	☐	☐	☐
Oven / Stove	☐	☐	☐
Microwave	☐	☐	☐
Layout	☐	☐	☐
Light Fixtures	☐	☐	☐
Backsplash	☐	☐	☐
Pantry	☐	☐	☐
Appliances	☐	☐	☐
Island	☐	☐	☐

	Good	Average	Poor
Basement	☐	☐	☐
Garage	☐	☐	☐

COMMUNITY

	Good	Average	Poor
Immediate Neighborhood	☐	☐	☐
Close to Employment	☐	☐	☐
Close to Shopping	☐	☐	☐
Close to Transportation	☐	☐	☐
Close to Schools / Daycare	☐	☐	☐
Close to Places of Worship	☐	☐	☐
Near Recreational Facilities	☐	☐	☐
Close to Airport	☐	☐	☐
Near Police and Fire Department	☐	☐	☐

Address ______________________ Price ____________

Bedrooms ____________ Bathrooms ____________ Sq.Ft. ____________

Lot Size: ____________ Year Built ____________ School District ________

Annual Tax ____________

EXTERIOR

	Good	Average	Poor
View/Yard/Landscaping	☐	☐	☐
Trees	☐	☐	☐
Lawn (Front)	☐	☐	☐
Lawn (Back)	☐	☐	☐
Fences (condition)	☐	☐	☐
Landscaping (condition)	☐	☐	☐
Irrigation / Sprinkler	☐	☐	☐
	☐	☐	☐
House Type	☐	☐	☐
Exterior Siding	☐	☐	☐
Deck / Patio / Porch	☐	☐	☐
Garage	☐	☐	☐
Window / Doors	☐	☐	☐
Roof / Gutters	☐	☐	☐
Fencing	☐	☐	☐

HOME SYSTEMS

	Good	Average	Poor
Electrical	☐	☐	☐
Air Conditioning / Fans	☐	☐	☐
Heating	☐	☐	☐
Security	☐	☐	☐
Plumbing	☐	☐	☐
Intercom	☐	☐	☐

FEATURES

	Good	Average	Poor
Home Warranty	☐	☐	☐
Energy Saving Features	☐	☐	☐

INTERIOR

	Good	Average	Poor
Walls / Trim / Ceilings	☐	☐	☐
Flooring	☐	☐	☐
Stairs	☐	☐	☐
Storage	☐	☐	☐
Living Room	☐	☐	☐
Family Room	☐	☐	☐
Dining Room	☐	☐	☐

	Good	Average	Poor
Master Bedroom	☐	☐	☐
Bedroom 2	☐	☐	☐
Bedroom 3	☐	☐	☐
Bedroom 4	☐	☐	☐
Master Bathroom	☐	☐	☐
Bathroom 2	☐	☐	☐
Bathroom 3	☐	☐	☐
Bonus / Game Room	☐	☐	☐

	Good	Average	Poor
Kitchen	☐	☐	☐
Cabinets	☐	☐	☐
Countertop	☐	☐	☐
Counter Space	☐	☐	☐
Flooring	☐	☐	☐
Oven / Stove	☐	☐	☐
Microwave	☐	☐	☐
Layout	☐	☐	☐
Light Fixtures	☐	☐	☐
Backsplash	☐	☐	☐
Pantry	☐	☐	☐
Appliances	☐	☐	☐
Island	☐	☐	☐

	Good	Average	Poor
Basement	☐	☐	☐
Garage	☐	☐	☐

COMMUNITY

	Good	Average	Poor
Immediate Neighborhood	☐	☐	☐
Close to Employment	☐	☐	☐
Close to Shopping	☐	☐	☐
Close to Transportation	☐	☐	☐
Close to Schools / Daycare	☐	☐	☐
Close to Places of Worship	☐	☐	☐
Near Recreational Facilities	☐	☐	☐
Close to Airport	☐	☐	☐
Near Police and Fire Department	☐	☐	☐

Address ____________________ Price ____________

Bedrooms __________ Bathrooms __________ Sq.Ft. ____________

Lot Size: __________ Year Built __________ School District __________

Annual Tax __________

EXTERIOR

	Good	Average	Poor
View/Yard/Landscaping	☐	☐	☐
Trees	☐	☐	☐
Lawn (Front)	☐	☐	☐
Lawn (Back)	☐	☐	☐
Fences (condition)	☐	☐	☐
Landscaping (condition)	☐	☐	☐
Irrigation / Sprinkler	☐	☐	☐
	☐	☐	☐
House Type	☐	☐	☐
Exterior Siding	☐	☐	☐
Deck / Patio / Porch	☐	☐	☐
Garage	☐	☐	☐
Window / Doors	☐	☐	☐
Roof / Gutters	☐	☐	☐
Fencing	☐	☐	☐

HOME SYSTEMS

	Good	Average	Poor
Electrical	☐	☐	☐
Air Conditioning / Fans	☐	☐	☐
Heating	☐	☐	☐
Security	☐	☐	☐
Plumbing	☐	☐	☐
Intercom	☐	☐	☐

FEATURES

	Good	Average	Poor
Home Warranty	☐	☐	☐
Energy Saving Features	☐	☐	☐

INTERIOR

	Good	Average	Poor
Walls / Trim / Ceilings	☐	☐	☐
Flooring	☐	☐	☐
Stairs	☐	☐	☐
Storage	☐	☐	☐
Living Room	☐	☐	☐
Family Room	☐	☐	☐
Dining Room	☐	☐	☐

	Good	Average	Poor
Master Bedroom	☐	☐	☐
Bedroom 2	☐	☐	☐
Bedroom 3	☐	☐	☐
Bedroom 4	☐	☐	☐
Master Bathroom	☐	☐	☐
Bathroom 2	☐	☐	☐
Bathroom 3	☐	☐	☐
Bonus / Game Room	☐	☐	☐

	Good	Average	Poor
Kitchen	☐	☐	☐
Cabinets	☐	☐	☐
Countertop	☐	☐	☐
Counter Space	☐	☐	☐
Flooring	☐	☐	☐
Oven / Stove	☐	☐	☐
Microwave	☐	☐	☐
Layout	☐	☐	☐
Light Fixtures	☐	☐	☐
Backsplash	☐	☐	☐
Pantry	☐	☐	☐
Appliances	☐	☐	☐
Island	☐	☐	☐

	Good	Average	Poor
Basement	☐	☐	☐
Garage	☐	☐	☐

COMMUNITY

	Good	Average	Poor
Immediate Neighborhood	☐	☐	☐
Close to Employment	☐	☐	☐
Close to Shopping	☐	☐	☐
Close to Transportation	☐	☐	☐
Close to Schools / Daycare	☐	☐	☐
Close to Places of Worship	☐	☐	☐
Near Recreational Facilities	☐	☐	☐
Close to Airport	☐	☐	☐
Near Police and Fire Department	☐	☐	☐

Address ______________________________ Price ______________

Bedrooms __________ Bathrooms __________ Sq.Ft. ______________

Lot Size: __________ Year Built __________ School District ______

Annual Tax __________

EXTERIOR

	Good	Average	Poor
View/Yard/Landscaping			
Trees			
Lawn (Front)			
Lawn (Back)			
Fences (condition)			
Landscaping (condition)			
Irrigation / Sprinkler			
House Type			
Exterior Siding			
Deck / Patio / Porch			
Garage			
Window / Doors			
Roof / Gutters			
Fencing			

HOME SYSTEMS

	Good	Average	Poor
Electrical			
Air Conditioning / Fans			
Heating			
Security			
Plumbing			
Intercom			

FEATURES

	Good	Average	Poor
Home Warranty			
Energy Saving Features			

INTERIOR

	Good	Average	Poor
Walls / Trim / Ceilings			
Flooring			
Stairs			
Storage			
Living Room			
Family Room			
Dining Room			

	Good	Average	Poor
Master Bedroom			
Bedroom 2			
Bedroom 3			
Bedroom 4			
Master Bathroom			
Bathroom 2			
Bathroom 3			
Bonus / Game Room			

	Good	Average	Poor
Kitchen			
Cabinets			
Countertop			
Counter Space			
Flooring			
Oven / Stove			
Microwave			
Layout			
Light Fixtures			
Backsplash			
Pantry			
Appliances			
Island			

	Good	Average	Poor
Basement			
Garage			

COMMUNITY

	Good	Average	Poor
Immediate Neighborhood			
Close to Employment			
Close to Shopping			
Close to Transportation			
Close to Schools / Daycare			
Close to Places of Worship			
Near Recreational Facilities			
Close to Airport			
Near Police and Fire Department			

Address ______________________ Price ______________

Bedrooms __________ Bathrooms __________ Sq.Ft. ______________

Lot Size: __________ Year Built __________ School District ________

Annual Tax __________

EXTERIOR

	Good	Average	Poor
View/Yard/Landscaping	☐	☐	☐
Trees	☐	☐	☐
Lawn (Front)	☐	☐	☐
Lawn (Back)	☐	☐	☐
Fences (condition)	☐	☐	☐
Landscaping (condition)	☐	☐	☐
Irrigation / Sprinkler	☐	☐	☐
	☐	☐	☐
House Type	☐	☐	☐
Exterior Siding	☐	☐	☐
Deck / Patio / Porch	☐	☐	☐
Garage	☐	☐	☐
Window / Doors	☐	☐	☐
Roof / Gutters	☐	☐	☐
Fencing	☐	☐	☐

HOME SYSTEMS

	Good	Average	Poor
Electrical	☐	☐	☐
Air Conditioning / Fans	☐	☐	☐
Heating	☐	☐	☐
Security	☐	☐	☐
Plumbing	☐	☐	☐
Intercom	☐	☐	☐

FEATURES

	Good	Average	Poor
Home Warranty	☐	☐	☐
Energy Saving Features	☐	☐	☐

INTERIOR

	Good	Average	Poor
Walls / Trim / Ceilings	☐	☐	☐
Flooring	☐	☐	☐
Stairs	☐	☐	☐
Storage	☐	☐	☐
Living Room	☐	☐	☐
Family Room	☐	☐	☐
Dining Room	☐	☐	☐

	Good	Average	Poor
Master Bedroom	☐	☐	☐
Bedroom 2	☐	☐	☐
Bedroom 3	☐	☐	☐
Bedroom 4	☐	☐	☐
Master Bathroom	☐	☐	☐
Bathroom 2	☐	☐	☐
Bathroom 3	☐	☐	☐
Bonus / Game Room	☐	☐	☐

	Good	Average	Poor
Kitchen	☐	☐	☐
Cabinets	☐	☐	☐
Countertop	☐	☐	☐
Counter Space	☐	☐	☐
Flooring	☐	☐	☐
Oven / Stove	☐	☐	☐
Microwave	☐	☐	☐
Layout	☐	☐	☐
Light Fixtures	☐	☐	☐
Backsplash	☐	☐	☐
Pantry	☐	☐	☐
Appliances	☐	☐	☐
Island	☐	☐	☐

	Good	Average	Poor
Basement	☐	☐	☐
Garage	☐	☐	☐

COMMUNITY

	Good	Average	Poor
Immediate Neighborhood	☐	☐	☐
Close to Employment	☐	☐	☐
Close to Shopping	☐	☐	☐
Close to Transportation	☐	☐	☐
Close to Schools / Daycare	☐	☐	☐
Close to Places of Worship	☐	☐	☐
Near Recreational Facilities	☐	☐	☐
Close to Airport	☐	☐	☐
Near Police and Fire Department	☐	☐	☐

Address ______________________ Price ______________

Bedrooms __________ Bathrooms __________ Sq.Ft. ______________

Lot Size: __________ Year Built __________ School District __________

Annual Tax __________

EXTERIOR

	Good	Average	Poor
View/Yard/Landscaping	☐	☐	☐
Trees	☐	☐	☐
Lawn (Front)	☐	☐	☐
Lawn (Back)	☐	☐	☐
Fences (condition)	☐	☐	☐
Landscaping (condition)	☐	☐	☐
Irrigation / Sprinkler	☐	☐	☐
	☐	☐	☐
House Type	☐	☐	☐
Exterior Siding	☐	☐	☐
Deck / Patio / Porch	☐	☐	☐
Garage	☐	☐	☐
Window / Doors	☐	☐	☐
Roof / Gutters	☐	☐	☐
Fencing	☐	☐	☐

HOME SYSTEMS

	Good	Average	Poor
Electrical	☐	☐	☐
Air Conditioning / Fans	☐	☐	☐
Heating	☐	☐	☐
Security	☐	☐	☐
Plumbing	☐	☐	☐
Intercom	☐	☐	☐

FEATURES

	Good	Average	Poor
Home Warranty	☐	☐	☐
Energy Saving Features	☐	☐	☐

INTERIOR

	Good	Average	Poor
Walls / Trim / Ceilings	☐	☐	☐
Flooring	☐	☐	☐
Stairs	☐	☐	☐
Storage	☐	☐	☐
Living Room	☐	☐	☐
Family Room	☐	☐	☐
Dining Room	☐	☐	☐

	Good	Average	Poor
Master Bedroom	☐	☐	☐
Bedroom 2	☐	☐	☐
Bedroom 3	☐	☐	☐
Bedroom 4	☐	☐	☐
Master Bathroom	☐	☐	☐
Bathroom 2	☐	☐	☐
Bathroom 3	☐	☐	☐
Bonus / Game Room	☐	☐	☐

	Good	Average	Poor
Kitchen	☐	☐	☐
Cabinets	☐	☐	☐
Countertop	☐	☐	☐
Counter Space	☐	☐	☐
Flooring	☐	☐	☐
Oven / Stove	☐	☐	☐
Microwave	☐	☐	☐
Layout	☐	☐	☐
Light Fixtures	☐	☐	☐
Backsplash	☐	☐	☐
Pantry	☐	☐	☐
Appliances	☐	☐	☐
Island	☐	☐	☐

	Good	Average	Poor
Basement	☐	☐	☐
Garage	☐	☐	☐

COMMUNITY

	Good	Average	Poor
Immediate Neighborhood	☐	☐	☐
Close to Employment	☐	☐	☐
Close to Shopping	☐	☐	☐
Close to Transportation	☐	☐	☐
Close to Schools / Daycare	☐	☐	☐
Close to Places of Worship	☐	☐	☐
Near Recreational Facilities	☐	☐	☐
Close to Airport	☐	☐	☐
Near Police and Fire Department	☐	☐	☐

Address ______________________ Price ______________

Bedrooms __________ Bathrooms __________ Sq.Ft. ______________

Lot Size: __________ Year Built __________ School District ________

Annual Tax __________

EXTERIOR

	Good	Average	Poor
View/Yard/Landscaping	☐	☐	☐
Trees	☐	☐	☐
Lawn (Front)	☐	☐	☐
Lawn (Back)	☐	☐	☐
Fences (condition)	☐	☐	☐
Landscaping (condition)	☐	☐	☐
Irrigation / Sprinkler	☐	☐	☐
	☐	☐	☐
House Type	☐	☐	☐
Exterior Siding	☐	☐	☐
Deck / Patio / Porch	☐	☐	☐
Garage	☐	☐	☐
Window / Doors	☐	☐	☐
Roof / Gutters	☐	☐	☐
Fencing	☐	☐	☐

HOME SYSTEMS

	Good	Average	Poor
Electrical	☐	☐	☐
Air Conditioning / Fans	☐	☐	☐
Heating	☐	☐	☐
Security	☐	☐	☐
Plumbing	☐	☐	☐
Intercom	☐	☐	☐

FEATURES

	Good	Average	Poor
Home Warranty	☐	☐	☐
Energy Saving Features	☐	☐	☐

INTERIOR

	Good	Average	Poor
Walls / Trim / Ceilings	☐	☐	☐
Flooring	☐	☐	☐
Stairs	☐	☐	☐
Storage	☐	☐	☐
Living Room	☐	☐	☐
Family Room	☐	☐	☐
Dining Room	☐	☐	☐

	Good	Average	Poor
Master Bedroom	☐	☐	☐
Bedroom 2	☐	☐	☐
Bedroom 3	☐	☐	☐
Bedroom 4	☐	☐	☐
Master Bathroom	☐	☐	☐
Bathroom 2	☐	☐	☐
Bathroom 3	☐	☐	☐
Bonus / Game Room	☐	☐	☐

	Good	Average	Poor
Kitchen	☐	☐	☐
Cabinets	☐	☐	☐
Countertop	☐	☐	☐
Counter Space	☐	☐	☐
Flooring	☐	☐	☐
Oven / Stove	☐	☐	☐
Microwave	☐	☐	☐
Layout	☐	☐	☐
Light Fixtures	☐	☐	☐
Backsplash	☐	☐	☐
Pantry	☐	☐	☐
Appliances	☐	☐	☐
Island	☐	☐	☐

	Good	Average	Poor
Basement	☐	☐	☐
Garage	☐	☐	☐

COMMUNITY

	Good	Average	Poor
Immediate Neighborhood	☐	☐	☐
Close to Employment	☐	☐	☐
Close to Shopping	☐	☐	☐
Close to Transportation	☐	☐	☐
Close to Schools / Daycare	☐	☐	☐
Close to Places of Worship	☐	☐	☐
Near Recreational Facilities	☐	☐	☐
Close to Airport	☐	☐	☐
Near Police and Fire Department	☐	☐	☐

Address ______________________ Price ______________

Bedrooms ____________ Bathrooms ____________ Sq.Ft. ______________

Lot Size: ____________ Year Built ____________ School District ________

Annual Tax ____________

EXTERIOR

	Good	Average	Poor
View/Yard/Landscaping	☐	☐	☐
Trees	☐	☐	☐
Lawn (Front)	☐	☐	☐
Lawn (Back)	☐	☐	☐
Fences (condition)	☐	☐	☐
Landscaping (condition)	☐	☐	☐
Irrigation / Sprinkler	☐	☐	☐
	☐	☐	☐
House Type	☐	☐	☐
Exterior Siding	☐	☐	☐
Deck / Patio / Porch	☐	☐	☐
Garage	☐	☐	☐
Window / Doors	☐	☐	☐
Roof / Gutters	☐	☐	☐
Fencing	☐	☐	☐

HOME SYSTEMS

	Good	Average	Poor
Electrical	☐	☐	☐
Air Conditioning / Fans	☐	☐	☐
Heating	☐	☐	☐
Security	☐	☐	☐
Plumbing	☐	☐	☐
Intercom	☐	☐	☐

FEATURES

	Good	Average	Poor
Home Warranty	☐	☐	☐
Energy Saving Features	☐	☐	☐

INTERIOR

	Good	Average	Poor
Walls / Trim / Ceilings	☐	☐	☐
Flooring	☐	☐	☐
Stairs	☐	☐	☐
Storage	☐	☐	☐
Living Room	☐	☐	☐
Family Room	☐	☐	☐
Dining Room	☐	☐	☐

	Good	Average	Poor
Master Bedroom	☐	☐	☐
Bedroom 2	☐	☐	☐
Bedroom 3	☐	☐	☐
Bedroom 4	☐	☐	☐
Master Bathroom	☐	☐	☐
Bathroom 2	☐	☐	☐
Bathroom 3	☐	☐	☐
Bonus / Game Room	☐	☐	☐

	Good	Average	Poor
Kitchen	☐	☐	☐
Cabinets	☐	☐	☐
Countertop	☐	☐	☐
Counter Space	☐	☐	☐
Flooring	☐	☐	☐
Oven / Stove	☐	☐	☐
Microwave	☐	☐	☐
Layout	☐	☐	☐
Light Fixtures	☐	☐	☐
Backsplash	☐	☐	☐
Pantry	☐	☐	☐
Appliances	☐	☐	☐
Island	☐	☐	☐

	Good	Average	Poor
Basement	☐	☐	☐
Garage	☐	☐	☐

COMMUNITY

	Good	Average	Poor
Immediate Neighborhood	☐	☐	☐
Close to Employment	☐	☐	☐
Close to Shopping	☐	☐	☐
Close to Transportation	☐	☐	☐
Close to Schools / Daycare	☐	☐	☐
Close to Places of Worship	☐	☐	☐
Near Recreational Facilities	☐	☐	☐
Close to Airport	☐	☐	☐
Near Police and Fire Department	☐	☐	☐

Address ______________________________ Price ______________

Bedrooms __________ Bathrooms __________ Sq.Ft. ______________

Lot Size: __________ Year Built __________ School District ________

Annual Tax __________

EXTERIOR

	Good	Average	Poor
View/Yard/Landscaping	☐	☐	☐
Trees	☐	☐	☐
Lawn (Front)	☐	☐	☐
Lawn (Back)	☐	☐	☐
Fences (condition)	☐	☐	☐
Landscaping (condition)	☐	☐	☐
Irrigation / Sprinkler	☐	☐	☐
	☐	☐	☐
House Type	☐	☐	☐
Exterior Siding	☐	☐	☐
Deck / Patio / Porch	☐	☐	☐
Garage	☐	☐	☐
Window / Doors	☐	☐	☐
Roof / Gutters	☐	☐	☐
Fencing	☐	☐	☐

HOME SYSTEMS

	Good	Average	Poor
Electrical	☐	☐	☐
Air Conditioning / Fans	☐	☐	☐
Heating	☐	☐	☐
Security	☐	☐	☐
Plumbing	☐	☐	☐
Intercom	☐	☐	☐

FEATURES

	Good	Average	Poor
Home Warranty	☐	☐	☐
Energy Saving Features	☐	☐	☐

INTERIOR

	Good	Average	Poor
Walls / Trim / Ceilings	☐	☐	☐
Flooring	☐	☐	☐
Stairs	☐	☐	☐
Storage	☐	☐	☐
Living Room	☐	☐	☐
Family Room	☐	☐	☐
Dining Room	☐	☐	☐

	Good	Average	Poor
Master Bedroom	☐	☐	☐
Bedroom 2	☐	☐	☐
Bedroom 3	☐	☐	☐
Bedroom 4	☐	☐	☐
Master Bathroom	☐	☐	☐
Bathroom 2	☐	☐	☐
Bathroom 3	☐	☐	☐
Bonus / Game Room	☐	☐	☐

	Good	Average	Poor
Kitchen	☐	☐	☐
Cabinets	☐	☐	☐
Countertop	☐	☐	☐
Counter Space	☐	☐	☐
Flooring	☐	☐	☐
Oven / Stove	☐	☐	☐
Microwave	☐	☐	☐
Layout	☐	☐	☐
Light Fixtures	☐	☐	☐
Backsplash	☐	☐	☐
Pantry	☐	☐	☐
Appliances	☐	☐	☐
Island	☐	☐	☐

	Good	Average	Poor
Basement	☐	☐	☐
Garage	☐	☐	☐

COMMUNITY

	Good	Average	Poor
Immediate Neighborhood	☐	☐	☐
Close to Employment	☐	☐	☐
Close to Shopping	☐	☐	☐
Close to Transportation	☐	☐	☐
Close to Schools / Daycare	☐	☐	☐
Close to Places of Worship	☐	☐	☐
Near Recreational Facilities	☐	☐	☐
Close to Airport	☐	☐	☐
Near Police and Fire Department	☐	☐	☐

Address ______________________ Price ______________

Bedrooms __________ Bathrooms __________ Sq.Ft. ______________

Lot Size: __________ Year Built __________ School District __________

Annual Tax __________

EXTERIOR

	Good	Average	Poor
View/Yard/Landscaping	☐	☐	☐
Trees	☐	☐	☐
Lawn (Front)	☐	☐	☐
Lawn (Back)	☐	☐	☐
Fences (condition)	☐	☐	☐
Landscaping (condition)	☐	☐	☐
Irrigation / Sprinkler	☐	☐	☐
	☐	☐	☐
House Type	☐	☐	☐
Exterior Siding	☐	☐	☐
Deck / Patio / Porch	☐	☐	☐
Garage	☐	☐	☐
Window / Doors	☐	☐	☐
Roof / Gutters	☐	☐	☐
Fencing	☐	☐	☐

HOME SYSTEMS

	Good	Average	Poor
Electrical	☐	☐	☐
Air Conditioning / Fans	☐	☐	☐
Heating	☐	☐	☐
Security	☐	☐	☐
Plumbing	☐	☐	☐
Intercom	☐	☐	☐

FEATURES

	Good	Average	Poor
Home Warranty	☐	☐	☐
Energy Saving Features	☐	☐	☐

INTERIOR

	Good	Average	Poor
Walls / Trim / Ceilings	☐	☐	☐
Flooring	☐	☐	☐
Stairs	☐	☐	☐
Storage	☐	☐	☐
Living Room	☐	☐	☐
Family Room	☐	☐	☐
Dining Room	☐	☐	☐

	Good	Average	Poor
Master Bedroom	☐	☐	☐
Bedroom 2	☐	☐	☐
Bedroom 3	☐	☐	☐
Bedroom 4	☐	☐	☐
Master Bathroom	☐	☐	☐
Bathroom 2	☐	☐	☐
Bathroom 3	☐	☐	☐
Bonus / Game Room	☐	☐	☐

	Good	Average	Poor
Kitchen	☐	☐	☐
Cabinets	☐	☐	☐
Countertop	☐	☐	☐
Counter Space	☐	☐	☐
Flooring	☐	☐	☐
Oven / Stove	☐	☐	☐
Microwave	☐	☐	☐
Layout	☐	☐	☐
Light Fixtures	☐	☐	☐
Backsplash	☐	☐	☐
Pantry	☐	☐	☐
Appliances	☐	☐	☐
Island	☐	☐	☐

	Good	Average	Poor
Basement	☐	☐	☐
Garage	☐	☐	☐

COMMUNITY

	Good	Average	Poor
Immediate Neighborhood	☐	☐	☐
Close to Employment	☐	☐	☐
Close to Shopping	☐	☐	☐
Close to Transportation	☐	☐	☐
Close to Schools / Daycare	☐	☐	☐
Close to Places of Worship	☐	☐	☐
Near Recreational Facilities	☐	☐	☐
Close to Airport	☐	☐	☐
Near Police and Fire Department	☐	☐	☐

Address ______________________ Price ______________

Bedrooms __________ Bathrooms __________ Sq.Ft. ______________

Lot Size: __________ Year Built __________ School District ________

Annual Tax __________

EXTERIOR

	Good	Average	Poor
View/Yard/Landscaping	☐	☐	☐
Trees	☐	☐	☐
Lawn (Front)	☐	☐	☐
Lawn (Back)	☐	☐	☐
Fences (condition)	☐	☐	☐
Landscaping (condition)	☐	☐	☐
Irrigation / Sprinkler	☐	☐	☐
	☐	☐	☐
House Type	☐	☐	☐
Exterior Siding	☐	☐	☐
Deck / Patio / Porch	☐	☐	☐
Garage	☐	☐	☐
Window / Doors	☐	☐	☐
Roof / Gutters	☐	☐	☐
Fencing	☐	☐	☐

HOME SYSTEMS

	Good	Average	Poor
Electrical	☐	☐	☐
Air Conditioning / Fans	☐	☐	☐
Heating	☐	☐	☐
Security	☐	☐	☐
Plumbing	☐	☐	☐
Intercom	☐	☐	☐

FEATURES

	Good	Average	Poor
Home Warranty	☐	☐	☐
Energy Saving Features	☐	☐	☐

INTERIOR

	Good	Average	Poor
Walls / Trim / Ceilings	☐	☐	☐
Flooring	☐	☐	☐
Stairs	☐	☐	☐
Storage	☐	☐	☐
Living Room	☐	☐	☐
Family Room	☐	☐	☐
Dining Room	☐	☐	☐

	Good	Average	Poor
Master Bedroom	☐	☐	☐
Bedroom 2	☐	☐	☐
Bedroom 3	☐	☐	☐
Bedroom 4	☐	☐	☐
Master Bathroom	☐	☐	☐
Bathroom 2	☐	☐	☐
Bathroom 3	☐	☐	☐
Bonus / Game Room	☐	☐	☐

	Good	Average	Poor
Kitchen	☐	☐	☐
Cabinets	☐	☐	☐
Countertop	☐	☐	☐
Counter Space	☐	☐	☐
Flooring	☐	☐	☐
Oven / Stove	☐	☐	☐
Microwave	☐	☐	☐
Layout	☐	☐	☐
Light Fixtures	☐	☐	☐
Backsplash	☐	☐	☐
Pantry	☐	☐	☐
Appliances	☐	☐	☐
Island	☐	☐	☐

	Good	Average	Poor
Basement	☐	☐	☐
Garage	☐	☐	☐

COMMUNITY

	Good	Average	Poor
Immediate Neighborhood	☐	☐	☐
Close to Employment	☐	☐	☐
Close to Shopping	☐	☐	☐
Close to Transportation	☐	☐	☐
Close to Schools / Daycare	☐	☐	☐
Close to Places of Worship	☐	☐	☐
Near Recreational Facilities	☐	☐	☐
Close to Airport	☐	☐	☐
Near Police and Fire Department	☐	☐	☐

Address ______________________________ Price ______________

Bedrooms __________ Bathrooms __________ Sq.Ft. ______________

Lot Size: __________ Year Built __________ School District ________

Annual Tax __________

EXTERIOR

	Good	Average	Poor
View/Yard/Landscaping			
Trees			
Lawn (Front)			
Lawn (Back)			
Fences (condition)			
Landscaping (condition)			
Irrigation / Sprinkler			
House Type			
Exterior Siding			
Deck / Patio / Porch			
Garage			
Window / Doors			
Roof / Gutters			
Fencing			

HOME SYSTEMS

	Good	Average	Poor
Electrical			
Air Conditioning / Fans			
Heating			
Security			
Plumbing			
Intercom			

FEATURES

	Good	Average	Poor
Home Warranty			
Energy Saving Features			

INTERIOR

	Good	Average	Poor
Walls / Trim / Ceilings			
Flooring			
Stairs			
Storage			
Living Room			
Family Room			
Dining Room			

	Good	Average	Poor
Master Bedroom			
Bedroom 2			
Bedroom 3			
Bedroom 4			
Master Bathroom			
Bathroom 2			
Bathroom 3			
Bonus / Game Room			

	Good	Average	Poor
Kitchen			
Cabinets			
Countertop			
Counter Space			
Flooring			
Oven / Stove			
Microwave			
Layout			
Light Fixtures			
Backsplash			
Pantry			
Appliances			
Island			

	Good	Average	Poor
Basement			
Garage			

COMMUNITY

	Good	Average	Poor
Immediate Neighborhood			
Close to Employment			
Close to Shopping			
Close to Transportation			
Close to Schools / Daycare			
Close to Places of Worship			
Near Recreational Facilities			
Close to Airport			
Near Police and Fire Department			

Address ____________________ Price ____________

Bedrooms ____________ Bathrooms ____________ Sq.Ft. ____________

Lot Size: ____________ Year Built ____________ School District ________

Annual Tax ____________

EXTERIOR

	Good	Average	Poor
View/Yard/Landscaping	☐	☐	☐
Trees	☐	☐	☐
Lawn (Front)	☐	☐	☐
Lawn (Back)	☐	☐	☐
Fences (condition)	☐	☐	☐
Landscaping (condition)	☐	☐	☐
Irrigation / Sprinkler	☐	☐	☐
	☐	☐	☐
House Type	☐	☐	☐
Exterior Siding	☐	☐	☐
Deck / Patio / Porch	☐	☐	☐
Garage	☐	☐	☐
Window / Doors	☐	☐	☐
Roof / Gutters	☐	☐	☐
Fencing	☐	☐	☐

HOME SYSTEMS

	Good	Average	Poor
Electrical	☐	☐	☐
Air Conditioning / Fans	☐	☐	☐
Heating	☐	☐	☐
Security	☐	☐	☐
Plumbing	☐	☐	☐
Intercom	☐	☐	☐

FEATURES

	Good	Average	Poor
Home Warranty	☐	☐	☐
Energy Saving Features	☐	☐	☐

INTERIOR

	Good	Average	Poor
Walls / Trim / Ceilings	☐	☐	☐
Flooring	☐	☐	☐
Stairs	☐	☐	☐
Storage	☐	☐	☐
Living Room	☐	☐	☐
Family Room	☐	☐	☐
Dining Room	☐	☐	☐

	Good	Average	Poor
Master Bedroom	☐	☐	☐
Bedroom 2	☐	☐	☐
Bedroom 3	☐	☐	☐
Bedroom 4	☐	☐	☐
Master Bathroom	☐	☐	☐
Bathroom 2	☐	☐	☐
Bathroom 3	☐	☐	☐
Bonus / Game Room	☐	☐	☐

	Good	Average	Poor
Kitchen	☐	☐	☐
Cabinets	☐	☐	☐
Countertop	☐	☐	☐
Counter Space	☐	☐	☐
Flooring	☐	☐	☐
Oven / Stove	☐	☐	☐
Microwave	☐	☐	☐
Layout	☐	☐	☐
Light Fixtures	☐	☐	☐
Backsplash	☐	☐	☐
Pantry	☐	☐	☐
Appliances	☐	☐	☐
Island	☐	☐	☐

	Good	Average	Poor
Basement	☐	☐	☐
Garage	☐	☐	☐

COMMUNITY

	Good	Average	Poor
Immediate Neighborhood	☐	☐	☐
Close to Employment	☐	☐	☐
Close to Shopping	☐	☐	☐
Close to Transportation	☐	☐	☐
Close to Schools / Daycare	☐	☐	☐
Close to Places of Worship	☐	☐	☐
Near Recreational Facilities	☐	☐	☐
Close to Airport	☐	☐	☐
Near Police and Fire Department	☐	☐	☐

Address ______________________ Price ____________

Bedrooms ________ Bathrooms ________ Sq.Ft. ____________

Lot Size: ________ Year Built ________ School District ________

Annual Tax ________

EXTERIOR

	Good	Average	Poor
View/Yard/Landscaping	☐	☐	☐
Trees	☐	☐	☐
Lawn (Front)	☐	☐	☐
Lawn (Back)	☐	☐	☐
Fences (condition)	☐	☐	☐
Landscaping (condition)	☐	☐	☐
Irrigation / Sprinkler	☐	☐	☐
	☐	☐	☐
House Type	☐	☐	☐
Exterior Siding	☐	☐	☐
Deck / Patio / Porch	☐	☐	☐
Garage	☐	☐	☐
Window / Doors	☐	☐	☐
Roof / Gutters	☐	☐	☐
Fencing	☐	☐	☐

HOME SYSTEMS

	Good	Average	Poor
Electrical	☐	☐	☐
Air Conditioning / Fans	☐	☐	☐
Heating	☐	☐	☐
Security	☐	☐	☐
Plumbing	☐	☐	☐
Intercom	☐	☐	☐

FEATURES

	Good	Average	Poor
Home Warranty	☐	☐	☐
Energy Saving Features	☐	☐	☐

INTERIOR

	Good	Average	Poor
Walls / Trim / Ceilings	☐	☐	☐
Flooring	☐	☐	☐
Stairs	☐	☐	☐
Storage	☐	☐	☐
Living Room	☐	☐	☐
Family Room	☐	☐	☐
Dining Room	☐	☐	☐

	Good	Average	Poor
Master Bedroom	☐	☐	☐
Bedroom 2	☐	☐	☐
Bedroom 3	☐	☐	☐
Bedroom 4	☐	☐	☐
Master Bathroom	☐	☐	☐
Bathroom 2	☐	☐	☐
Bathroom 3	☐	☐	☐
Bonus / Game Room	☐	☐	☐

	Good	Average	Poor
Kitchen	☐	☐	☐
Cabinets	☐	☐	☐
Countertop	☐	☐	☐
Counter Space	☐	☐	☐
Flooring	☐	☐	☐
Oven / Stove	☐	☐	☐
Microwave	☐	☐	☐
Layout	☐	☐	☐
Light Fixtures	☐	☐	☐
Backsplash	☐	☐	☐
Pantry	☐	☐	☐
Appliances	☐	☐	☐
Island	☐	☐	☐

	Good	Average	Poor
Basement	☐	☐	☐
Garage	☐	☐	☐

COMMUNITY

	Good	Average	Poor
Immediate Neighborhood	☐	☐	☐
Close to Employment	☐	☐	☐
Close to Shopping	☐	☐	☐
Close to Transportation	☐	☐	☐
Close to Schools / Daycare	☐	☐	☐
Close to Places of Worship	☐	☐	☐
Near Recreational Facilities	☐	☐	☐
Close to Airport	☐	☐	☐
Near Police and Fire Department	☐	☐	☐

Address ______________________ Price ______________

Bedrooms __________ Bathrooms __________ Sq.Ft. ______________

Lot Size: __________ Year Built __________ School District ______

Annual Tax __________

EXTERIOR

	Good	Average	Poor
View/Yard/Landscaping	☐	☐	☐
Trees	☐	☐	☐
Lawn (Front)	☐	☐	☐
Lawn (Back)	☐	☐	☐
Fences (condition)	☐	☐	☐
Landscaping (condition)	☐	☐	☐
Irrigation / Sprinkler	☐	☐	☐
	☐	☐	☐
House Type	☐	☐	☐
Exterior Siding	☐	☐	☐
Deck / Patio / Porch	☐	☐	☐
Garage	☐	☐	☐
Window / Doors	☐	☐	☐
Roof / Gutters	☐	☐	☐
Fencing	☐	☐	☐

HOME SYSTEMS

	Good	Average	Poor
Electrical	☐	☐	☐
Air Conditioning / Fans	☐	☐	☐
Heating	☐	☐	☐
Security	☐	☐	☐
Plumbing	☐	☐	☐
Intercom	☐	☐	☐

FEATURES

	Good	Average	Poor
Home Warranty	☐	☐	☐
Energy Saving Features	☐	☐	☐

INTERIOR

	Good	Average	Poor
Walls / Trim / Ceilings	☐	☐	☐
Flooring	☐	☐	☐
Stairs	☐	☐	☐
Storage	☐	☐	☐
Living Room	☐	☐	☐
Family Room	☐	☐	☐
Dining Room	☐	☐	☐

	Good	Average	Poor
Master Bedroom	☐	☐	☐
Bedroom 2	☐	☐	☐
Bedroom 3	☐	☐	☐
Bedroom 4	☐	☐	☐
Master Bathroom	☐	☐	☐
Bathroom 2	☐	☐	☐
Bathroom 3	☐	☐	☐
Bonus / Game Room	☐	☐	☐

	Good	Average	Poor
Kitchen	☐	☐	☐
Cabinets	☐	☐	☐
Countertop	☐	☐	☐
Counter Space	☐	☐	☐
Flooring	☐	☐	☐
Oven / Stove	☐	☐	☐
Microwave	☐	☐	☐
Layout	☐	☐	☐
Light Fixtures	☐	☐	☐
Backsplash	☐	☐	☐
Pantry	☐	☐	☐
Appliances	☐	☐	☐
Island	☐	☐	☐

	Good	Average	Poor
Basement	☐	☐	☐
Garage	☐	☐	☐

COMMUNITY

	Good	Average	Poor
Immediate Neighborhood	☐	☐	☐
Close to Employment	☐	☐	☐
Close to Shopping	☐	☐	☐
Close to Transportation	☐	☐	☐
Close to Schools / Daycare	☐	☐	☐
Close to Places of Worship	☐	☐	☐
Near Recreational Facilities	☐	☐	☐
Close to Airport	☐	☐	☐
Near Police and Fire Department	☐	☐	☐

Address ______________________ Price ____________

Bedrooms ________ Bathrooms ________ Sq.Ft. ____________

Lot Size: ________ Year Built ________ School District ________

Annual Tax ________

EXTERIOR

	Good	Average	Poor
View/Yard/Landscaping	☐	☐	☐
Trees	☐	☐	☐
Lawn (Front)	☐	☐	☐
Lawn (Back)	☐	☐	☐
Fences (condition)	☐	☐	☐
Landscaping (condition)	☐	☐	☐
Irrigation / Sprinkler	☐	☐	☐
	☐	☐	☐
House Type	☐	☐	☐
Exterior Siding	☐	☐	☐
Deck / Patio / Porch	☐	☐	☐
Garage	☐	☐	☐
Window / Doors	☐	☐	☐
Roof / Gutters	☐	☐	☐
Fencing	☐	☐	☐

HOME SYSTEMS

	Good	Average	Poor
Electrical	☐	☐	☐
Air Conditioning / Fans	☐	☐	☐
Heating	☐	☐	☐
Security	☐	☐	☐
Plumbing	☐	☐	☐
Intercom	☐	☐	☐

FEATURES

	Good	Average	Poor
Home Warranty	☐	☐	☐
Energy Saving Features	☐	☐	☐

INTERIOR

	Good	Average	Poor
Walls / Trim / Ceilings	☐	☐	☐
Flooring	☐	☐	☐
Stairs	☐	☐	☐
Storage	☐	☐	☐
Living Room	☐	☐	☐
Family Room	☐	☐	☐
Dining Room	☐	☐	☐

	Good	Average	Poor
Master Bedroom	☐	☐	☐
Bedroom 2	☐	☐	☐
Bedroom 3	☐	☐	☐
Bedroom 4	☐	☐	☐
Master Bathroom	☐	☐	☐
Bathroom 2	☐	☐	☐
Bathroom 3	☐	☐	☐
Bonus / Game Room	☐	☐	☐

	Good	Average	Poor
Kitchen	☐	☐	☐
Cabinets	☐	☐	☐
Countertop	☐	☐	☐
Counter Space	☐	☐	☐
Flooring	☐	☐	☐
Oven / Stove	☐	☐	☐
Microwave	☐	☐	☐
Layout	☐	☐	☐
Light Fixtures	☐	☐	☐
Backsplash	☐	☐	☐
Pantry	☐	☐	☐
Appliances	☐	☐	☐
Island	☐	☐	☐

	Good	Average	Poor
Basement	☐	☐	☐
Garage	☐	☐	☐

COMMUNITY

	Good	Average	Poor
Immediate Neighborhood	☐	☐	☐
Close to Employment	☐	☐	☐
Close to Shopping	☐	☐	☐
Close to Transportation	☐	☐	☐
Close to Schools / Daycare	☐	☐	☐
Close to Places of Worship	☐	☐	☐
Near Recreational Facilities	☐	☐	☐
Close to Airport	☐	☐	☐
Near Police and Fire Department	☐	☐	☐

Address ______________________ Price ______________

Bedrooms __________ Bathrooms __________ Sq.Ft. ______________

Lot Size: __________ Year Built __________ School District ______

Annual Tax __________

EXTERIOR

	Good	Average	Poor
View/Yard/Landscaping	☐	☐	☐
Trees	☐	☐	☐
Lawn (Front)	☐	☐	☐
Lawn (Back)	☐	☐	☐
Fences (condition)	☐	☐	☐
Landscaping (condition)	☐	☐	☐
Irrigation / Sprinkler	☐	☐	☐
	☐	☐	☐
House Type	☐	☐	☐
Exterior Siding	☐	☐	☐
Deck / Patio / Porch	☐	☐	☐
Garage	☐	☐	☐
Window / Doors	☐	☐	☐
Roof / Gutters	☐	☐	☐
Fencing	☐	☐	☐

HOME SYSTEMS

	Good	Average	Poor
Electrical	☐	☐	☐
Air Conditioning / Fans	☐	☐	☐
Heating	☐	☐	☐
Security	☐	☐	☐
Plumbing	☐	☐	☐
Intercom	☐	☐	☐

FEATURES

	Good	Average	Poor
Home Warranty	☐	☐	☐
Energy Saving Features	☐	☐	☐

INTERIOR

	Good	Average	Poor
Walls / Trim / Ceilings	☐	☐	☐
Flooring	☐	☐	☐
Stairs	☐	☐	☐
Storage	☐	☐	☐
Living Room	☐	☐	☐
Family Room	☐	☐	☐
Dining Room	☐	☐	☐

	Good	Average	Poor
Master Bedroom	☐	☐	☐
Bedroom 2	☐	☐	☐
Bedroom 3	☐	☐	☐
Bedroom 4	☐	☐	☐
Master Bathroom	☐	☐	☐
Bathroom 2	☐	☐	☐
Bathroom 3	☐	☐	☐
Bonus / Game Room	☐	☐	☐

	Good	Average	Poor
Kitchen	☐	☐	☐
Cabinets	☐	☐	☐
Countertop	☐	☐	☐
Counter Space	☐	☐	☐
Flooring	☐	☐	☐
Oven / Stove	☐	☐	☐
Microwave	☐	☐	☐
Layout	☐	☐	☐
Light Fixtures	☐	☐	☐
Backsplash	☐	☐	☐
Pantry	☐	☐	☐
Appliances	☐	☐	☐
Island	☐	☐	☐

	Good	Average	Poor
Basement	☐	☐	☐
Garage	☐	☐	☐

COMMUNITY

	Good	Average	Poor
Immediate Neighborhood	☐	☐	☐
Close to Employment	☐	☐	☐
Close to Shopping	☐	☐	☐
Close to Transportation	☐	☐	☐
Close to Schools / Daycare	☐	☐	☐
Close to Places of Worship	☐	☐	☐
Near Recreational Facilities	☐	☐	☐
Close to Airport	☐	☐	☐
Near Police and Fire Department	☐	☐	☐

Address ______________________ Price ____________

Bedrooms ________ Bathrooms ________ Sq.Ft. ____________

Lot Size: ________ Year Built ________ School District ________

Annual Tax ________

EXTERIOR

	Good	Average	Poor
View/Yard/Landscaping	☐	☐	☐
Trees	☐	☐	☐
Lawn (Front)	☐	☐	☐
Lawn (Back)	☐	☐	☐
Fences (condition)	☐	☐	☐
Landscaping (condition)	☐	☐	☐
Irrigation / Sprinkler	☐	☐	☐
	☐	☐	☐
House Type	☐	☐	☐
Exterior Siding	☐	☐	☐
Deck / Patio / Porch	☐	☐	☐
Garage	☐	☐	☐
Window / Doors	☐	☐	☐
Roof / Gutters	☐	☐	☐
Fencing	☐	☐	☐

HOME SYSTEMS

	Good	Average	Poor
Electrical	☐	☐	☐
Air Conditioning / Fans	☐	☐	☐
Heating	☐	☐	☐
Security	☐	☐	☐
Plumbing	☐	☐	☐
Intercom	☐	☐	☐

FEATURES

	Good	Average	Poor
Home Warranty	☐	☐	☐
Energy Saving Features	☐	☐	☐

INTERIOR

	Good	Average	Poor
Walls / Trim / Ceilings	☐	☐	☐
Flooring	☐	☐	☐
Stairs	☐	☐	☐
Storage	☐	☐	☐
Living Room	☐	☐	☐
Family Room	☐	☐	☐
Dining Room	☐	☐	☐

	Good	Average	Poor
Master Bedroom	☐	☐	☐
Bedroom 2	☐	☐	☐
Bedroom 3	☐	☐	☐
Bedroom 4	☐	☐	☐
Master Bathroom	☐	☐	☐
Bathroom 2	☐	☐	☐
Bathroom 3	☐	☐	☐
Bonus / Game Room	☐	☐	☐

	Good	Average	Poor
Kitchen	☐	☐	☐
Cabinets	☐	☐	☐
Countertop	☐	☐	☐
Counter Space	☐	☐	☐
Flooring	☐	☐	☐
Oven / Stove	☐	☐	☐
Microwave	☐	☐	☐
Layout	☐	☐	☐
Light Fixtures	☐	☐	☐
Backsplash	☐	☐	☐
Pantry	☐	☐	☐
Appliances	☐	☐	☐
Island	☐	☐	☐

	Good	Average	Poor
Basement	☐	☐	☐
Garage	☐	☐	☐

COMMUNITY

	Good	Average	Poor
Immediate Neighborhood	☐	☐	☐
Close to Employment	☐	☐	☐
Close to Shopping	☐	☐	☐
Close to Transportation	☐	☐	☐
Close to Schools / Daycare	☐	☐	☐
Close to Places of Worship	☐	☐	☐
Near Recreational Facilities	☐	☐	☐
Close to Airport	☐	☐	☐
Near Police and Fire Department	☐	☐	☐

Address ______________________ Price ____________

Bedrooms ________ Bathrooms ________ Sq.Ft. ____________

Lot Size: ________ Year Built ________ School District ________

Annual Tax ________

EXTERIOR

	Good	Average	Poor
View/Yard/Landscaping	☐	☐	☐
Trees	☐	☐	☐
Lawn (Front)	☐	☐	☐
Lawn (Back)	☐	☐	☐
Fences (condition)	☐	☐	☐
Landscaping (condition)	☐	☐	☐
Irrigation / Sprinkler	☐	☐	☐
	☐	☐	☐
House Type	☐	☐	☐
Exterior Siding	☐	☐	☐
Deck / Patio / Porch	☐	☐	☐
Garage	☐	☐	☐
Window / Doors	☐	☐	☐
Roof / Gutters	☐	☐	☐
Fencing	☐	☐	☐

HOME SYSTEMS

	Good	Average	Poor
Electrical	☐	☐	☐
Air Conditioning / Fans	☐	☐	☐
Heating	☐	☐	☐
Security	☐	☐	☐
Plumbing	☐	☐	☐
Intercom	☐	☐	☐

FEATURES

	Good	Average	Poor
Home Warranty	☐	☐	☐
Energy Saving Features	☐	☐	☐

INTERIOR

	Good	Average	Poor
Walls / Trim / Ceilings	☐	☐	☐
Flooring	☐	☐	☐
Stairs	☐	☐	☐
Storage	☐	☐	☐
Living Room	☐	☐	☐
Family Room	☐	☐	☐
Dining Room	☐	☐	☐

	Good	Average	Poor
Master Bedroom	☐	☐	☐
Bedroom 2	☐	☐	☐
Bedroom 3	☐	☐	☐
Bedroom 4	☐	☐	☐
Master Bathroom	☐	☐	☐
Bathroom 2	☐	☐	☐
Bathroom 3	☐	☐	☐
Bonus / Game Room	☐	☐	☐

	Good	Average	Poor
Kitchen	☐	☐	☐
Cabinets	☐	☐	☐
Countertop	☐	☐	☐
Counter Space	☐	☐	☐
Flooring	☐	☐	☐
Oven / Stove	☐	☐	☐
Microwave	☐	☐	☐
Layout	☐	☐	☐
Light Fixtures	☐	☐	☐
Backsplash	☐	☐	☐
Pantry	☐	☐	☐
Appliances	☐	☐	☐
Island	☐	☐	☐

	Good	Average	Poor
Basement	☐	☐	☐
Garage	☐	☐	☐

COMMUNITY

	Good	Average	Poor
Immediate Neighborhood	☐	☐	☐
Close to Employment	☐	☐	☐
Close to Shopping	☐	☐	☐
Close to Transportation	☐	☐	☐
Close to Schools / Daycare	☐	☐	☐
Close to Places of Worship	☐	☐	☐
Near Recreational Facilities	☐	☐	☐
Close to Airport	☐	☐	☐
Near Police and Fire Department	☐	☐	☐

Address ______________________ Price ____________

Bedrooms ________ Bathrooms ________ Sq.Ft. ____________

Lot Size: ________ Year Built ________ School District ______

Annual Tax ________

EXTERIOR

	Good	Average	Poor
View/Yard/Landscaping	☐	☐	☐
Trees	☐	☐	☐
Lawn (Front)	☐	☐	☐
Lawn (Back)	☐	☐	☐
Fences (condition)	☐	☐	☐
Landscaping (condition)	☐	☐	☐
Irrigation / Sprinkler	☐	☐	☐
	☐	☐	☐
House Type	☐	☐	☐
Exterior Siding	☐	☐	☐
Deck / Patio / Porch	☐	☐	☐
Garage	☐	☐	☐
Window / Doors	☐	☐	☐
Roof / Gutters	☐	☐	☐
Fencing	☐	☐	☐

HOME SYSTEMS

	Good	Average	Poor
Electrical	☐	☐	☐
Air Conditioning / Fans	☐	☐	☐
Heating	☐	☐	☐
Security	☐	☐	☐
Plumbing	☐	☐	☐
Intercom	☐	☐	☐

FEATURES

	Good	Average	Poor
Home Warranty	☐	☐	☐
Energy Saving Features	☐	☐	☐

INTERIOR

	Good	Average	Poor
Walls / Trim / Ceilings	☐	☐	☐
Flooring	☐	☐	☐
Stairs	☐	☐	☐
Storage	☐	☐	☐
Living Room	☐	☐	☐
Family Room	☐	☐	☐
Dining Room	☐	☐	☐

	Good	Average	Poor
Master Bedroom	☐	☐	☐
Bedroom 2	☐	☐	☐
Bedroom 3	☐	☐	☐
Bedroom 4	☐	☐	☐
Master Bathroom	☐	☐	☐
Bathroom 2	☐	☐	☐
Bathroom 3	☐	☐	☐
Bonus / Game Room	☐	☐	☐

	Good	Average	Poor
Kitchen	☐	☐	☐
Cabinets	☐	☐	☐
Countertop	☐	☐	☐
Counter Space	☐	☐	☐
Flooring	☐	☐	☐
Oven / Stove	☐	☐	☐
Microwave	☐	☐	☐
Layout	☐	☐	☐
Light Fixtures	☐	☐	☐
Backsplash	☐	☐	☐
Pantry	☐	☐	☐
Appliances	☐	☐	☐
Island	☐	☐	☐

	Good	Average	Poor
Basement	☐	☐	☐
Garage	☐	☐	☐

COMMUNITY

	Good	Average	Poor
Immediate Neighborhood	☐	☐	☐
Close to Employment	☐	☐	☐
Close to Shopping	☐	☐	☐
Close to Transportation	☐	☐	☐
Close to Schools / Daycare	☐	☐	☐
Close to Places of Worship	☐	☐	☐
Near Recreational Facilities	☐	☐	☐
Close to Airport	☐	☐	☐
Near Police and Fire Department	☐	☐	☐

Address ______________________ Price ______________

Bedrooms __________ Bathrooms __________ Sq.Ft. ______________

Lot Size: __________ Year Built __________ School District ________

Annual Tax __________

EXTERIOR

	Good	Average	Poor
View/Yard/Landscaping	☐	☐	☐
Trees	☐	☐	☐
Lawn (Front)	☐	☐	☐
Lawn (Back)	☐	☐	☐
Fences (condition)	☐	☐	☐
Landscaping (condition)	☐	☐	☐
Irrigation / Sprinkler	☐	☐	☐
	☐	☐	☐
House Type	☐	☐	☐
Exterior Siding	☐	☐	☐
Deck / Patio / Porch	☐	☐	☐
Garage	☐	☐	☐
Window / Doors	☐	☐	☐
Roof / Gutters	☐	☐	☐
Fencing	☐	☐	☐

HOME SYSTEMS

	Good	Average	Poor
Electrical	☐	☐	☐
Air Conditioning / Fans	☐	☐	☐
Heating	☐	☐	☐
Security	☐	☐	☐
Plumbing	☐	☐	☐
Intercom	☐	☐	☐

FEATURES

	Good	Average	Poor
Home Warranty	☐	☐	☐
Energy Saving Features	☐	☐	☐

INTERIOR

	Good	Average	Poor
Walls / Trim / Ceilings	☐	☐	☐
Flooring	☐	☐	☐
Stairs	☐	☐	☐
Storage	☐	☐	☐
Living Room	☐	☐	☐
Family Room	☐	☐	☐
Dining Room	☐	☐	☐

	Good	Average	Poor
Master Bedroom	☐	☐	☐
Bedroom 2	☐	☐	☐
Bedroom 3	☐	☐	☐
Bedroom 4	☐	☐	☐
Master Bathroom	☐	☐	☐
Bathroom 2	☐	☐	☐
Bathroom 3	☐	☐	☐
Bonus / Game Room	☐	☐	☐

	Good	Average	Poor
Kitchen	☐	☐	☐
Cabinets	☐	☐	☐
Countertop	☐	☐	☐
Counter Space	☐	☐	☐
Flooring	☐	☐	☐
Oven / Stove	☐	☐	☐
Microwave	☐	☐	☐
Layout	☐	☐	☐
Light Fixtures	☐	☐	☐
Backsplash	☐	☐	☐
Pantry	☐	☐	☐
Appliances	☐	☐	☐
Island	☐	☐	☐

	Good	Average	Poor
Basement	☐	☐	☐
Garage	☐	☐	☐

COMMUNITY

	Good	Average	Poor
Immediate Neighborhood	☐	☐	☐
Close to Employment	☐	☐	☐
Close to Shopping	☐	☐	☐
Close to Transportation	☐	☐	☐
Close to Schools / Daycare	☐	☐	☐
Close to Places of Worship	☐	☐	☐
Near Recreational Facilities	☐	☐	☐
Close to Airport	☐	☐	☐
Near Police and Fire Department	☐	☐	☐

Address ______________________ Price ____________

Bedrooms ____________ Bathrooms ____________ Sq.Ft. ____________

Lot Size: ____________ Year Built ____________ School District ________

Annual Tax ____________

EXTERIOR

	Good	Average	Poor
View/Yard/Landscaping	☐	☐	☐
Trees	☐	☐	☐
Lawn (Front)	☐	☐	☐
Lawn (Back)	☐	☐	☐
Fences (condition)	☐	☐	☐
Landscaping (condition)	☐	☐	☐
Irrigation / Sprinkler	☐	☐	☐
	☐	☐	☐
House Type	☐	☐	☐
Exterior Siding	☐	☐	☐
Deck / Patio / Porch	☐	☐	☐
Garage	☐	☐	☐
Window / Doors	☐	☐	☐
Roof / Gutters	☐	☐	☐
Fencing	☐	☐	☐

HOME SYSTEMS

	Good	Average	Poor
Electrical	☐	☐	☐
Air Conditioning / Fans	☐	☐	☐
Heating	☐	☐	☐
Security	☐	☐	☐
Plumbing	☐	☐	☐
Intercom	☐	☐	☐

FEATURES

	Good	Average	Poor
Home Warranty	☐	☐	☐
Energy Saving Features	☐	☐	☐

INTERIOR

	Good	Average	Poor
Walls / Trim / Ceilings	☐	☐	☐
Flooring	☐	☐	☐
Stairs	☐	☐	☐
Storage	☐	☐	☐
Living Room	☐	☐	☐
Family Room	☐	☐	☐
Dining Room	☐	☐	☐

	Good	Average	Poor
Master Bedroom	☐	☐	☐
Bedroom 2	☐	☐	☐
Bedroom 3	☐	☐	☐
Bedroom 4	☐	☐	☐
Master Bathroom	☐	☐	☐
Bathroom 2	☐	☐	☐
Bathroom 3	☐	☐	☐
Bonus / Game Room	☐	☐	☐

	Good	Average	Poor
Kitchen	☐	☐	☐
Cabinets	☐	☐	☐
Countertop	☐	☐	☐
Counter Space	☐	☐	☐
Flooring	☐	☐	☐
Oven / Stove	☐	☐	☐
Microwave	☐	☐	☐
Layout	☐	☐	☐
Light Fixtures	☐	☐	☐
Backsplash	☐	☐	☐
Pantry	☐	☐	☐
Appliances	☐	☐	☐
Island	☐	☐	☐

	Good	Average	Poor
Basement	☐	☐	☐
Garage	☐	☐	☐

COMMUNITY

	Good	Average	Poor
Immediate Neighborhood	☐	☐	☐
Close to Employment	☐	☐	☐
Close to Shopping	☐	☐	☐
Close to Transportation	☐	☐	☐
Close to Schools / Daycare	☐	☐	☐
Close to Places of Worship	☐	☐	☐
Near Recreational Facilities	☐	☐	☐
Close to Airport	☐	☐	☐
Near Police and Fire Department	☐	☐	☐

Address ______________________ Price ______________

Bedrooms __________ Bathrooms __________ Sq.Ft. ______________

Lot Size: __________ Year Built __________ School District ______

Annual Tax __________

EXTERIOR

	Good	Average	Poor
View/Yard/Landscaping	☐	☐	☐
Trees	☐	☐	☐
Lawn (Front)	☐	☐	☐
Lawn (Back)	☐	☐	☐
Fences (condition)	☐	☐	☐
Landscaping (condition)	☐	☐	☐
Irrigation / Sprinkler	☐	☐	☐
	☐	☐	☐
House Type	☐	☐	☐
Exterior Siding	☐	☐	☐
Deck / Patio / Porch	☐	☐	☐
Garage	☐	☐	☐
Window / Doors	☐	☐	☐
Roof / Gutters	☐	☐	☐
Fencing	☐	☐	☐

HOME SYSTEMS

	Good	Average	Poor
Electrical	☐	☐	☐
Air Conditioning / Fans	☐	☐	☐
Heating	☐	☐	☐
Security	☐	☐	☐
Plumbing	☐	☐	☐
Intercom	☐	☐	☐

FEATURES

	Good	Average	Poor
Home Warranty	☐	☐	☐
Energy Saving Features	☐	☐	☐

INTERIOR

	Good	Average	Poor
Walls / Trim / Ceilings	☐	☐	☐
Flooring	☐	☐	☐
Stairs	☐	☐	☐
Storage	☐	☐	☐
Living Room	☐	☐	☐
Family Room	☐	☐	☐
Dining Room	☐	☐	☐

	Good	Average	Poor
Master Bedroom	☐	☐	☐
Bedroom 2	☐	☐	☐
Bedroom 3	☐	☐	☐
Bedroom 4	☐	☐	☐
Master Bathroom	☐	☐	☐
Bathroom 2	☐	☐	☐
Bathroom 3	☐	☐	☐
Bonus / Game Room	☐	☐	☐

	Good	Average	Poor
Kitchen	☐	☐	☐
Cabinets	☐	☐	☐
Countertop	☐	☐	☐
Counter Space	☐	☐	☐
Flooring	☐	☐	☐
Oven / Stove	☐	☐	☐
Microwave	☐	☐	☐
Layout	☐	☐	☐
Light Fixtures	☐	☐	☐
Backsplash	☐	☐	☐
Pantry	☐	☐	☐
Appliances	☐	☐	☐
Island	☐	☐	☐

	Good	Average	Poor
Basement	☐	☐	☐
Garage	☐	☐	☐

COMMUNITY

	Good	Average	Poor
Immediate Neighborhood	☐	☐	☐
Close to Employment	☐	☐	☐
Close to Shopping	☐	☐	☐
Close to Transportation	☐	☐	☐
Close to Schools / Daycare	☐	☐	☐
Close to Places of Worship	☐	☐	☐
Near Recreational Facilities	☐	☐	☐
Close to Airport	☐	☐	☐
Near Police and Fire Department	☐	☐	☐

Address ______________________ Price ______________

Bedrooms __________ Bathrooms __________ Sq.Ft. ______________

Lot Size: __________ Year Built __________ School District ______

Annual Tax __________

EXTERIOR

	Good	Average	Poor
View/Yard/Landscaping	☐	☐	☐
Trees	☐	☐	☐
Lawn (Front)	☐	☐	☐
Lawn (Back)	☐	☐	☐
Fences (condition)	☐	☐	☐
Landscaping (condition)	☐	☐	☐
Irrigation / Sprinkler	☐	☐	☐
	☐	☐	☐
House Type	☐	☐	☐
Exterior Siding	☐	☐	☐
Deck / Patio / Porch	☐	☐	☐
Garage	☐	☐	☐
Window / Doors	☐	☐	☐
Roof / Gutters	☐	☐	☐
Fencing	☐	☐	☐

HOME SYSTEMS

	Good	Average	Poor
Electrical	☐	☐	☐
Air Conditioning / Fans	☐	☐	☐
Heating	☐	☐	☐
Security	☐	☐	☐
Plumbing	☐	☐	☐
Intercom	☐	☐	☐

FEATURES

	Good	Average	Poor
Home Warranty	☐	☐	☐
Energy Saving Features	☐	☐	☐

INTERIOR

	Good	Average	Poor
Walls / Trim / Ceilings	☐	☐	☐
Flooring	☐	☐	☐
Stairs	☐	☐	☐
Storage	☐	☐	☐
Living Room	☐	☐	☐
Family Room	☐	☐	☐
Dining Room	☐	☐	☐

	Good	Average	Poor
Master Bedroom	☐	☐	☐
Bedroom 2	☐	☐	☐
Bedroom 3	☐	☐	☐
Bedroom 4	☐	☐	☐
Master Bathroom	☐	☐	☐
Bathroom 2	☐	☐	☐
Bathroom 3	☐	☐	☐
Bonus / Game Room	☐	☐	☐

	Good	Average	Poor
Kitchen	☐	☐	☐
Cabinets	☐	☐	☐
Countertop	☐	☐	☐
Counter Space	☐	☐	☐
Flooring	☐	☐	☐
Oven / Stove	☐	☐	☐
Microwave	☐	☐	☐
Layout	☐	☐	☐
Light Fixtures	☐	☐	☐
Backsplash	☐	☐	☐
Pantry	☐	☐	☐
Appliances	☐	☐	☐
Island	☐	☐	☐

	Good	Average	Poor
Basement	☐	☐	☐
Garage	☐	☐	☐

COMMUNITY

	Good	Average	Poor
Immediate Neighborhood	☐	☐	☐
Close to Employment	☐	☐	☐
Close to Shopping	☐	☐	☐
Close to Transportation	☐	☐	☐
Close to Schools / Daycare	☐	☐	☐
Close to Places of Worship	☐	☐	☐
Near Recreational Facilities	☐	☐	☐
Close to Airport	☐	☐	☐
Near Police and Fire Department	☐	☐	☐

Address ______________________ Price ____________

Bedrooms ________ Bathrooms ________ Sq.Ft. ____________

Lot Size: ________ Year Built ________ School District ________

Annual Tax ________

EXTERIOR

	Good	Average	Poor
View/Yard/Landscaping	☐	☐	☐
Trees	☐	☐	☐
Lawn (Front)	☐	☐	☐
Lawn (Back)	☐	☐	☐
Fences (condition)	☐	☐	☐
Landscaping (condition)	☐	☐	☐
Irrigation / Sprinkler	☐	☐	☐
	☐	☐	☐
House Type	☐	☐	☐
Exterior Siding	☐	☐	☐
Deck / Patio / Porch	☐	☐	☐
Garage	☐	☐	☐
Window / Doors	☐	☐	☐
Roof / Gutters	☐	☐	☐
Fencing	☐	☐	☐

HOME SYSTEMS

	Good	Average	Poor
Electrical	☐	☐	☐
Air Conditioning / Fans	☐	☐	☐
Heating	☐	☐	☐
Security	☐	☐	☐
Plumbing	☐	☐	☐
Intercom	☐	☐	☐

FEATURES

	Good	Average	Poor
Home Warranty	☐	☐	☐
Energy Saving Features	☐	☐	☐

INTERIOR

	Good	Average	Poor
Walls / Trim / Ceilings	☐	☐	☐
Flooring	☐	☐	☐
Stairs	☐	☐	☐
Storage	☐	☐	☐
Living Room	☐	☐	☐
Family Room	☐	☐	☐
Dining Room	☐	☐	☐

	Good	Average	Poor
Master Bedroom	☐	☐	☐
Bedroom 2	☐	☐	☐
Bedroom 3	☐	☐	☐
Bedroom 4	☐	☐	☐
Master Bathroom	☐	☐	☐
Bathroom 2	☐	☐	☐
Bathroom 3	☐	☐	☐
Bonus / Game Room	☐	☐	☐

	Good	Average	Poor
Kitchen	☐	☐	☐
Cabinets	☐	☐	☐
Countertop	☐	☐	☐
Counter Space	☐	☐	☐
Flooring	☐	☐	☐
Oven / Stove	☐	☐	☐
Microwave	☐	☐	☐
Layout	☐	☐	☐
Light Fixtures	☐	☐	☐
Backsplash	☐	☐	☐
Pantry	☐	☐	☐
Appliances	☐	☐	☐
Island	☐	☐	☐

	Good	Average	Poor
Basement	☐	☐	☐
Garage	☐	☐	☐

COMMUNITY

	Good	Average	Poor
Immediate Neighborhood	☐	☐	☐
Close to Employment	☐	☐	☐
Close to Shopping	☐	☐	☐
Close to Transportation	☐	☐	☐
Close to Schools / Daycare	☐	☐	☐
Close to Places of Worship	☐	☐	☐
Near Recreational Facilities	☐	☐	☐
Close to Airport	☐	☐	☐
Near Police and Fire Department	☐	☐	☐

Address ______________________ Price ______________

Bedrooms ________ Bathrooms ________ Sq.Ft. ______________

Lot Size: ________ Year Built ________ School District ________

Annual Tax ________

EXTERIOR

	Good	Average	Poor
View/Yard/Landscaping	☐	☐	☐
Trees	☐	☐	☐
Lawn (Front)	☐	☐	☐
Lawn (Back)	☐	☐	☐
Fences (condition)	☐	☐	☐
Landscaping (condition)	☐	☐	☐
Irrigation / Sprinkler	☐	☐	☐
	☐	☐	☐
House Type	☐	☐	☐
Exterior Siding	☐	☐	☐
Deck / Patio / Porch	☐	☐	☐
Garage	☐	☐	☐
Window / Doors	☐	☐	☐
Roof / Gutters	☐	☐	☐
Fencing	☐	☐	☐

HOME SYSTEMS

	Good	Average	Poor
Electrical	☐	☐	☐
Air Conditioning / Fans	☐	☐	☐
Heating	☐	☐	☐
Security	☐	☐	☐
Plumbing	☐	☐	☐
Intercom	☐	☐	☐

FEATURES

	Good	Average	Poor
Home Warranty	☐	☐	☐
Energy Saving Features	☐	☐	☐

INTERIOR

	Good	Average	Poor
Walls / Trim / Ceilings	☐	☐	☐
Flooring	☐	☐	☐
Stairs	☐	☐	☐
Storage	☐	☐	☐
Living Room	☐	☐	☐
Family Room	☐	☐	☐
Dining Room	☐	☐	☐

	Good	Average	Poor
Master Bedroom	☐	☐	☐
Bedroom 2	☐	☐	☐
Bedroom 3	☐	☐	☐
Bedroom 4	☐	☐	☐
Master Bathroom	☐	☐	☐
Bathroom 2	☐	☐	☐
Bathroom 3	☐	☐	☐
Bonus / Game Room	☐	☐	☐

	Good	Average	Poor
Kitchen	☐	☐	☐
Cabinets	☐	☐	☐
Countertop	☐	☐	☐
Counter Space	☐	☐	☐
Flooring	☐	☐	☐
Oven / Stove	☐	☐	☐
Microwave	☐	☐	☐
Layout	☐	☐	☐
Light Fixtures	☐	☐	☐
Backsplash	☐	☐	☐
Pantry	☐	☐	☐
Appliances	☐	☐	☐
Island	☐	☐	☐

	Good	Average	Poor
Basement	☐	☐	☐
Garage	☐	☐	☐

COMMUNITY

	Good	Average	Poor
Immediate Neighborhood	☐	☐	☐
Close to Employment	☐	☐	☐
Close to Shopping	☐	☐	☐
Close to Transportation	☐	☐	☐
Close to Schools / Daycare	☐	☐	☐
Close to Places of Worship	☐	☐	☐
Near Recreational Facilities	☐	☐	☐
Close to Airport	☐	☐	☐
Near Police and Fire Department	☐	☐	☐

Address ______________________ Price ______________

Bedrooms __________ Bathrooms __________ Sq.Ft. ______________

Lot Size: __________ Year Built __________ School District __________

Annual Tax __________

EXTERIOR

	Good	Average	Poor
View/Yard/Landscaping	☐	☐	☐
Trees	☐	☐	☐
Lawn (Front)	☐	☐	☐
Lawn (Back)	☐	☐	☐
Fences (condition)	☐	☐	☐
Landscaping (condition)	☐	☐	☐
Irrigation / Sprinkler	☐	☐	☐
	☐	☐	☐
House Type	☐	☐	☐
Exterior Siding	☐	☐	☐
Deck / Patio / Porch	☐	☐	☐
Garage	☐	☐	☐
Window / Doors	☐	☐	☐
Roof / Gutters	☐	☐	☐
Fencing	☐	☐	☐

HOME SYSTEMS

	Good	Average	Poor
Electrical	☐	☐	☐
Air Conditioning / Fans	☐	☐	☐
Heating	☐	☐	☐
Security	☐	☐	☐
Plumbing	☐	☐	☐
Intercom	☐	☐	☐

FEATURES

	Good	Average	Poor
Home Warranty	☐	☐	☐
Energy Saving Features	☐	☐	☐

INTERIOR

	Good	Average	Poor
Walls / Trim / Ceilings	☐	☐	☐
Flooring	☐	☐	☐
Stairs	☐	☐	☐
Storage	☐	☐	☐
Living Room	☐	☐	☐
Family Room	☐	☐	☐
Dining Room	☐	☐	☐

	Good	Average	Poor
Master Bedroom	☐	☐	☐
Bedroom 2	☐	☐	☐
Bedroom 3	☐	☐	☐
Bedroom 4	☐	☐	☐
Master Bathroom	☐	☐	☐
Bathroom 2	☐	☐	☐
Bathroom 3	☐	☐	☐
Bonus / Game Room	☐	☐	☐

	Good	Average	Poor
Kitchen	☐	☐	☐
Cabinets	☐	☐	☐
Countertop	☐	☐	☐
Counter Space	☐	☐	☐
Flooring	☐	☐	☐
Oven / Stove	☐	☐	☐
Microwave	☐	☐	☐
Layout	☐	☐	☐
Light Fixtures	☐	☐	☐
Backsplash	☐	☐	☐
Pantry	☐	☐	☐
Appliances	☐	☐	☐
Island	☐	☐	☐

	Good	Average	Poor
Basement	☐	☐	☐
Garage	☐	☐	☐

COMMUNITY

	Good	Average	Poor
Immediate Neighborhood	☐	☐	☐
Close to Employment	☐	☐	☐
Close to Shopping	☐	☐	☐
Close to Transportation	☐	☐	☐
Close to Schools / Daycare	☐	☐	☐
Close to Places of Worship	☐	☐	☐
Near Recreational Facilities	☐	☐	☐
Close to Airport	☐	☐	☐
Near Police and Fire Department	☐	☐	☐

Address ______________________ Price ____________

Bedrooms ________ Bathrooms ________ Sq.Ft. ____________

Lot Size: ________ Year Built ________ School District ________

Annual Tax ________

EXTERIOR

	Good	Average	Poor
View/Yard/Landscaping	☐	☐	☐
Trees	☐	☐	☐
Lawn (Front)	☐	☐	☐
Lawn (Back)	☐	☐	☐
Fences (condition)	☐	☐	☐
Landscaping (condition)	☐	☐	☐
Irrigation / Sprinkler	☐	☐	☐
	☐	☐	☐
House Type	☐	☐	☐
Exterior Siding	☐	☐	☐
Deck / Patio / Porch	☐	☐	☐
Garage	☐	☐	☐
Window / Doors	☐	☐	☐
Roof / Gutters	☐	☐	☐
Fencing	☐	☐	☐

HOME SYSTEMS

	Good	Average	Poor
Electrical	☐	☐	☐
Air Conditioning / Fans	☐	☐	☐
Heating	☐	☐	☐
Security	☐	☐	☐
Plumbing	☐	☐	☐
Intercom	☐	☐	☐

FEATURES

	Good	Average	Poor
Home Warranty	☐	☐	☐
Energy Saving Features	☐	☐	☐

INTERIOR

	Good	Average	Poor
Walls / Trim / Ceilings	☐	☐	☐
Flooring	☐	☐	☐
Stairs	☐	☐	☐
Storage	☐	☐	☐
Living Room	☐	☐	☐
Family Room	☐	☐	☐
Dining Room	☐	☐	☐

	Good	Average	Poor
Master Bedroom	☐	☐	☐
Bedroom 2	☐	☐	☐
Bedroom 3	☐	☐	☐
Bedroom 4	☐	☐	☐
Master Bathroom	☐	☐	☐
Bathroom 2	☐	☐	☐
Bathroom 3	☐	☐	☐
Bonus / Game Room	☐	☐	☐

	Good	Average	Poor
Kitchen	☐	☐	☐
Cabinets	☐	☐	☐
Countertop	☐	☐	☐
Counter Space	☐	☐	☐
Flooring	☐	☐	☐
Oven / Stove	☐	☐	☐
Microwave	☐	☐	☐
Layout	☐	☐	☐
Light Fixtures	☐	☐	☐
Backsplash	☐	☐	☐
Pantry	☐	☐	☐
Appliances	☐	☐	☐
Island	☐	☐	☐

	Good	Average	Poor
Basement	☐	☐	☐
Garage	☐	☐	☐

COMMUNITY

	Good	Average	Poor
Immediate Neighborhood	☐	☐	☐
Close to Employment	☐	☐	☐
Close to Shopping	☐	☐	☐
Close to Transportation	☐	☐	☐
Close to Schools / Daycare	☐	☐	☐
Close to Places of Worship	☐	☐	☐
Near Recreational Facilities	☐	☐	☐
Close to Airport	☐	☐	☐
Near Police and Fire Department	☐	☐	☐

Address ____________________ Price ____________

Bedrooms ________ Bathrooms ________ Sq.Ft. ____________

Lot Size: ________ Year Built ________ School District ________

Annual Tax ________

EXTERIOR

	Good	Average	Poor
View/Yard/Landscaping	☐	☐	☐
Trees	☐	☐	☐
Lawn (Front)	☐	☐	☐
Lawn (Back)	☐	☐	☐
Fences (condition)	☐	☐	☐
Landscaping (condition)	☐	☐	☐
Irrigation / Sprinkler	☐	☐	☐
	☐	☐	☐
House Type	☐	☐	☐
Exterior Siding	☐	☐	☐
Deck / Patio / Porch	☐	☐	☐
Garage	☐	☐	☐
Window / Doors	☐	☐	☐
Roof / Gutters	☐	☐	☐
Fencing	☐	☐	☐

HOME SYSTEMS

	Good	Average	Poor
Electrical	☐	☐	☐
Air Conditioning / Fans	☐	☐	☐
Heating	☐	☐	☐
Security	☐	☐	☐
Plumbing	☐	☐	☐
Intercom	☐	☐	☐

FEATURES

	Good	Average	Poor
Home Warranty	☐	☐	☐
Energy Saving Features	☐	☐	☐

INTERIOR

	Good	Average	Poor
Walls / Trim / Ceilings	☐	☐	☐
Flooring	☐	☐	☐
Stairs	☐	☐	☐
Storage	☐	☐	☐
Living Room	☐	☐	☐
Family Room	☐	☐	☐
Dining Room	☐	☐	☐

	Good	Average	Poor
Master Bedroom	☐	☐	☐
Bedroom 2	☐	☐	☐
Bedroom 3	☐	☐	☐
Bedroom 4	☐	☐	☐
Master Bathroom	☐	☐	☐
Bathroom 2	☐	☐	☐
Bathroom 3	☐	☐	☐
Bonus / Game Room	☐	☐	☐

	Good	Average	Poor
Kitchen	☐	☐	☐
Cabinets	☐	☐	☐
Countertop	☐	☐	☐
Counter Space	☐	☐	☐
Flooring	☐	☐	☐
Oven / Stove	☐	☐	☐
Microwave	☐	☐	☐
Layout	☐	☐	☐
Light Fixtures	☐	☐	☐
Backsplash	☐	☐	☐
Pantry	☐	☐	☐
Appliances	☐	☐	☐
Island	☐	☐	☐

	Good	Average	Poor
Basement	☐	☐	☐
Garage	☐	☐	☐

COMMUNITY

	Good	Average	Poor
Immediate Neighborhood	☐	☐	☐
Close to Employment	☐	☐	☐
Close to Shopping	☐	☐	☐
Close to Transportation	☐	☐	☐
Close to Schools / Daycare	☐	☐	☐
Close to Places of Worship	☐	☐	☐
Near Recreational Facilities	☐	☐	☐
Close to Airport	☐	☐	☐
Near Police and Fire Department	☐	☐	☐

Address ____________________ Price ____________

Bedrooms ________ Bathrooms ________ Sq.Ft. ____________

Lot Size: ________ Year Built ________ School District ________

Annual Tax ________

EXTERIOR

	Good	Average	Poor
View/Yard/Landscaping	☐	☐	☐
Trees	☐	☐	☐
Lawn (Front)	☐	☐	☐
Lawn (Back)	☐	☐	☐
Fences (condition)	☐	☐	☐
Landscaping (condition)	☐	☐	☐
Irrigation / Sprinkler	☐	☐	☐
	☐	☐	☐
House Type	☐	☐	☐
Exterior Siding	☐	☐	☐
Deck / Patio / Porch	☐	☐	☐
Garage	☐	☐	☐
Window / Doors	☐	☐	☐
Roof / Gutters	☐	☐	☐
Fencing	☐	☐	☐

HOME SYSTEMS

	Good	Average	Poor
Electrical	☐	☐	☐
Air Conditioning / Fans	☐	☐	☐
Heating	☐	☐	☐
Security	☐	☐	☐
Plumbing	☐	☐	☐
Intercom	☐	☐	☐

FEATURES

	Good	Average	Poor
Home Warranty	☐	☐	☐
Energy Saving Features	☐	☐	☐

INTERIOR

	Good	Average	Poor
Walls / Trim / Ceilings	☐	☐	☐
Flooring	☐	☐	☐
Stairs	☐	☐	☐
Storage	☐	☐	☐
Living Room	☐	☐	☐
Family Room	☐	☐	☐
Dining Room	☐	☐	☐

	Good	Average	Poor
Master Bedroom	☐	☐	☐
Bedroom 2	☐	☐	☐
Bedroom 3	☐	☐	☐
Bedroom 4	☐	☐	☐
Master Bathroom	☐	☐	☐
Bathroom 2	☐	☐	☐
Bathroom 3	☐	☐	☐
Bonus / Game Room	☐	☐	☐

	Good	Average	Poor
Kitchen	☐	☐	☐
Cabinets	☐	☐	☐
Countertop	☐	☐	☐
Counter Space	☐	☐	☐
Flooring	☐	☐	☐
Oven / Stove	☐	☐	☐
Microwave	☐	☐	☐
Layout	☐	☐	☐
Light Fixtures	☐	☐	☐
Backsplash	☐	☐	☐
Pantry	☐	☐	☐
Appliances	☐	☐	☐
Island	☐	☐	☐

	Good	Average	Poor
Basement	☐	☐	☐
Garage	☐	☐	☐

COMMUNITY

	Good	Average	Poor
Immediate Neighborhood	☐	☐	☐
Close to Employment	☐	☐	☐
Close to Shopping	☐	☐	☐
Close to Transportation	☐	☐	☐
Close to Schools / Daycare	☐	☐	☐
Close to Places of Worship	☐	☐	☐
Near Recreational Facilities	☐	☐	☐
Close to Airport	☐	☐	☐
Near Police and Fire Department	☐	☐	☐

Address ______________________ Price ____________

Bedrooms ____________ Bathrooms ____________ Sq.Ft. ____________

Lot Size: ____________ Year Built ____________ School District ________

Annual Tax ____________

EXTERIOR

	Good	Average	Poor
View/Yard/Landscaping	☐	☐	☐
Trees	☐	☐	☐
Lawn (Front)	☐	☐	☐
Lawn (Back)	☐	☐	☐
Fences (condition)	☐	☐	☐
Landscaping (condition)	☐	☐	☐
Irrigation / Sprinkler	☐	☐	☐
	☐	☐	☐
House Type	☐	☐	☐
Exterior Siding	☐	☐	☐
Deck / Patio / Porch	☐	☐	☐
Garage	☐	☐	☐
Window / Doors	☐	☐	☐
Roof / Gutters	☐	☐	☐
Fencing	☐	☐	☐

HOME SYSTEMS

	Good	Average	Poor
Electrical	☐	☐	☐
Air Conditioning / Fans	☐	☐	☐
Heating	☐	☐	☐
Security	☐	☐	☐
Plumbing	☐	☐	☐
Intercom	☐	☐	☐

FEATURES

	Good	Average	Poor
Home Warranty	☐	☐	☐
Energy Saving Features	☐	☐	☐

INTERIOR

	Good	Average	Poor
Walls / Trim / Ceilings	☐	☐	☐
Flooring	☐	☐	☐
Stairs	☐	☐	☐
Storage	☐	☐	☐
Living Room	☐	☐	☐
Family Room	☐	☐	☐
Dining Room	☐	☐	☐

	Good	Average	Poor
Master Bedroom	☐	☐	☐
Bedroom 2	☐	☐	☐
Bedroom 3	☐	☐	☐
Bedroom 4	☐	☐	☐
Master Bathroom	☐	☐	☐
Bathroom 2	☐	☐	☐
Bathroom 3	☐	☐	☐
Bonus / Game Room	☐	☐	☐

	Good	Average	Poor
Kitchen	☐	☐	☐
Cabinets	☐	☐	☐
Countertop	☐	☐	☐
Counter Space	☐	☐	☐
Flooring	☐	☐	☐
Oven / Stove	☐	☐	☐
Microwave	☐	☐	☐
Layout	☐	☐	☐
Light Fixtures	☐	☐	☐
Backsplash	☐	☐	☐
Pantry	☐	☐	☐
Appliances	☐	☐	☐
Island	☐	☐	☐

	Good	Average	Poor
Basement	☐	☐	☐
Garage	☐	☐	☐

COMMUNITY

	Good	Average	Poor
Immediate Neighborhood	☐	☐	☐
Close to Employment	☐	☐	☐
Close to Shopping	☐	☐	☐
Close to Transportation	☐	☐	☐
Close to Schools / Daycare	☐	☐	☐
Close to Places of Worship	☐	☐	☐
Near Recreational Facilities	☐	☐	☐
Close to Airport	☐	☐	☐
Near Police and Fire Department	☐	☐	☐

Address ______________________ Price ____________

Bedrooms ____________ Bathrooms ____________ Sq.Ft. ____________

Lot Size: ____________ Year Built ____________ School District ________

Annual Tax ____________

EXTERIOR

	Good	Average	Poor
View/Yard/Landscaping	☐	☐	☐
Trees	☐	☐	☐
Lawn (Front)	☐	☐	☐
Lawn (Back)	☐	☐	☐
Fences (condition)	☐	☐	☐
Landscaping (condition)	☐	☐	☐
Irrigation / Sprinkler	☐	☐	☐
	☐	☐	☐
House Type	☐	☐	☐
Exterior Siding	☐	☐	☐
Deck / Patio / Porch	☐	☐	☐
Garage	☐	☐	☐
Window / Doors	☐	☐	☐
Roof / Gutters	☐	☐	☐
Fencing	☐	☐	☐

HOME SYSTEMS

	Good	Average	Poor
Electrical	☐	☐	☐
Air Conditioning / Fans	☐	☐	☐
Heating	☐	☐	☐
Security	☐	☐	☐
Plumbing	☐	☐	☐
Intercom	☐	☐	☐

FEATURES

	Good	Average	Poor
Home Warranty	☐	☐	☐
Energy Saving Features	☐	☐	☐

INTERIOR

	Good	Average	Poor
Walls / Trim / Ceilings	☐	☐	☐
Flooring	☐	☐	☐
Stairs	☐	☐	☐
Storage	☐	☐	☐
Living Room	☐	☐	☐
Family Room	☐	☐	☐
Dining Room	☐	☐	☐

	Good	Average	Poor
Master Bedroom	☐	☐	☐
Bedroom 2	☐	☐	☐
Bedroom 3	☐	☐	☐
Bedroom 4	☐	☐	☐
Master Bathroom	☐	☐	☐
Bathroom 2	☐	☐	☐
Bathroom 3	☐	☐	☐
Bonus / Game Room	☐	☐	☐

	Good	Average	Poor
Kitchen	☐	☐	☐
Cabinets	☐	☐	☐
Countertop	☐	☐	☐
Counter Space	☐	☐	☐
Flooring	☐	☐	☐
Oven / Stove	☐	☐	☐
Microwave	☐	☐	☐
Layout	☐	☐	☐
Light Fixtures	☐	☐	☐
Backsplash	☐	☐	☐
Pantry	☐	☐	☐
Appliances	☐	☐	☐
Island	☐	☐	☐

	Good	Average	Poor
Basement	☐	☐	☐
Garage	☐	☐	☐

COMMUNITY

	Good	Average	Poor
Immediate Neighborhood	☐	☐	☐
Close to Employment	☐	☐	☐
Close to Shopping	☐	☐	☐
Close to Transportation	☐	☐	☐
Close to Schools / Daycare	☐	☐	☐
Close to Places of Worship	☐	☐	☐
Near Recreational Facilities	☐	☐	☐
Close to Airport	☐	☐	☐
Near Police and Fire Department	☐	☐	☐

Address ______________________ Price ____________

Bedrooms ________ Bathrooms ________ Sq.Ft. ____________

Lot Size: ________ Year Built ________ School District ________

Annual Tax ________

EXTERIOR

	Good	Average	Poor
View/Yard/Landscaping	☐	☐	☐
Trees	☐	☐	☐
Lawn (Front)	☐	☐	☐
Lawn (Back)	☐	☐	☐
Fences (condition)	☐	☐	☐
Landscaping (condition)	☐	☐	☐
Irrigation / Sprinkler	☐	☐	☐
	☐	☐	☐
House Type	☐	☐	☐
Exterior Siding	☐	☐	☐
Deck / Patio / Porch	☐	☐	☐
Garage	☐	☐	☐
Window / Doors	☐	☐	☐
Roof / Gutters	☐	☐	☐
Fencing	☐	☐	☐

HOME SYSTEMS

	Good	Average	Poor
Electrical	☐	☐	☐
Air Conditioning / Fans	☐	☐	☐
Heating	☐	☐	☐
Security	☐	☐	☐
Plumbing	☐	☐	☐
Intercom	☐	☐	☐

FEATURES

	Good	Average	Poor
Home Warranty	☐	☐	☐
Energy Saving Features	☐	☐	☐

INTERIOR

	Good	Average	Poor
Walls / Trim / Ceilings	☐	☐	☐
Flooring	☐	☐	☐
Stairs	☐	☐	☐
Storage	☐	☐	☐
Living Room	☐	☐	☐
Family Room	☐	☐	☐
Dining Room	☐	☐	☐

	Good	Average	Poor
Master Bedroom	☐	☐	☐
Bedroom 2	☐	☐	☐
Bedroom 3	☐	☐	☐
Bedroom 4	☐	☐	☐
Master Bathroom	☐	☐	☐
Bathroom 2	☐	☐	☐
Bathroom 3	☐	☐	☐
Bonus / Game Room	☐	☐	☐

	Good	Average	Poor
Kitchen	☐	☐	☐
Cabinets	☐	☐	☐
Countertop	☐	☐	☐
Counter Space	☐	☐	☐
Flooring	☐	☐	☐
Oven / Stove	☐	☐	☐
Microwave	☐	☐	☐
Layout	☐	☐	☐
Light Fixtures	☐	☐	☐
Backsplash	☐	☐	☐
Pantry	☐	☐	☐
Appliances	☐	☐	☐
Island	☐	☐	☐

	Good	Average	Poor
Basement	☐	☐	☐
Garage	☐	☐	☐

COMMUNITY

	Good	Average	Poor
Immediate Neighborhood	☐	☐	☐
Close to Employment	☐	☐	☐
Close to Shopping	☐	☐	☐
Close to Transportation	☐	☐	☐
Close to Schools / Daycare	☐	☐	☐
Close to Places of Worship	☐	☐	☐
Near Recreational Facilities	☐	☐	☐
Close to Airport	☐	☐	☐
Near Police and Fire Department	☐	☐	☐

Address ______________________ Price ____________

Bedrooms __________ Bathrooms __________ Sq.Ft. ____________

Lot Size: __________ Year Built __________ School District ________

Annual Tax ________

EXTERIOR

	Good	Average	Poor
View/Yard/Landscaping	☐	☐	☐
Trees	☐	☐	☐
Lawn (Front)	☐	☐	☐
Lawn (Back)	☐	☐	☐
Fences (condition)	☐	☐	☐
Landscaping (condition)	☐	☐	☐
Irrigation / Sprinkler	☐	☐	☐
	☐	☐	☐
House Type	☐	☐	☐
Exterior Siding	☐	☐	☐
Deck / Patio / Porch	☐	☐	☐
Garage	☐	☐	☐
Window / Doors	☐	☐	☐
Roof / Gutters	☐	☐	☐
Fencing	☐	☐	☐

HOME SYSTEMS

	Good	Average	Poor
Electrical	☐	☐	☐
Air Conditioning / Fans	☐	☐	☐
Heating	☐	☐	☐
Security	☐	☐	☐
Plumbing	☐	☐	☐
Intercom	☐	☐	☐

FEATURES

	Good	Average	Poor
Home Warranty	☐	☐	☐
Energy Saving Features	☐	☐	☐

INTERIOR

	Good	Average	Poor
Walls / Trim / Ceilings	☐	☐	☐
Flooring	☐	☐	☐
Stairs	☐	☐	☐
Storage	☐	☐	☐
Living Room	☐	☐	☐
Family Room	☐	☐	☐
Dining Room	☐	☐	☐

	Good	Average	Poor
Master Bedroom	☐	☐	☐
Bedroom 2	☐	☐	☐
Bedroom 3	☐	☐	☐
Bedroom 4	☐	☐	☐
Master Bathroom	☐	☐	☐
Bathroom 2	☐	☐	☐
Bathroom 3	☐	☐	☐
Bonus / Game Room	☐	☐	☐

	Good	Average	Poor
Kitchen	☐	☐	☐
Cabinets	☐	☐	☐
Countertop	☐	☐	☐
Counter Space	☐	☐	☐
Flooring	☐	☐	☐
Oven / Stove	☐	☐	☐
Microwave	☐	☐	☐
Layout	☐	☐	☐
Light Fixtures	☐	☐	☐
Backsplash	☐	☐	☐
Pantry	☐	☐	☐
Appliances	☐	☐	☐
Island	☐	☐	☐

	Good	Average	Poor
Basement	☐	☐	☐
Garage	☐	☐	☐

COMMUNITY

	Good	Average	Poor
Immediate Neighborhood	☐	☐	☐
Close to Employment	☐	☐	☐
Close to Shopping	☐	☐	☐
Close to Transportation	☐	☐	☐
Close to Schools / Daycare	☐	☐	☐
Close to Places of Worship	☐	☐	☐
Near Recreational Facilities	☐	☐	☐
Close to Airport	☐	☐	☐
Near Police and Fire Department	☐	☐	☐

Address ______________________________ Price ______________

Bedrooms __________ Bathrooms __________ Sq.Ft. ______________

Lot Size: __________ Year Built __________ School District _______

Annual Tax __________

EXTERIOR

	Good	Average	Poor
View/Yard/Landscaping	☐	☐	☐
Trees	☐	☐	☐
Lawn (Front)	☐	☐	☐
Lawn (Back)	☐	☐	☐
Fences (condition)	☐	☐	☐
Landscaping (condition)	☐	☐	☐
Irrigation / Sprinkler	☐	☐	☐
	☐	☐	☐
House Type	☐	☐	☐
Exterior Siding	☐	☐	☐
Deck / Patio / Porch	☐	☐	☐
Garage	☐	☐	☐
Window / Doors	☐	☐	☐
Roof / Gutters	☐	☐	☐
Fencing	☐	☐	☐

HOME SYSTEMS

	Good	Average	Poor
Electrical	☐	☐	☐
Air Conditioning / Fans	☐	☐	☐
Heating	☐	☐	☐
Security	☐	☐	☐
Plumbing	☐	☐	☐
Intercom	☐	☐	☐

FEATURES

	Good	Average	Poor
Home Warranty	☐	☐	☐
Energy Saving Features	☐	☐	☐

INTERIOR

	Good	Average	Poor
Walls / Trim / Ceilings	☐	☐	☐
Flooring	☐	☐	☐
Stairs	☐	☐	☐
Storage	☐	☐	☐
Living Room	☐	☐	☐
Family Room	☐	☐	☐
Dining Room	☐	☐	☐

	Good	Average	Poor
Master Bedroom	☐	☐	☐
Bedroom 2	☐	☐	☐
Bedroom 3	☐	☐	☐
Bedroom 4	☐	☐	☐
Master Bathroom	☐	☐	☐
Bathroom 2	☐	☐	☐
Bathroom 3	☐	☐	☐
Bonus / Game Room	☐	☐	☐

	Good	Average	Poor
Kitchen	☐	☐	☐
Cabinets	☐	☐	☐
Countertop	☐	☐	☐
Counter Space	☐	☐	☐
Flooring	☐	☐	☐
Oven / Stove	☐	☐	☐
Microwave	☐	☐	☐
Layout	☐	☐	☐
Light Fixtures	☐	☐	☐
Backsplash	☐	☐	☐
Pantry	☐	☐	☐
Appliances	☐	☐	☐
Island	☐	☐	☐

	Good	Average	Poor
Basement	☐	☐	☐
Garage	☐	☐	☐

COMMUNITY

	Good	Average	Poor
Immediate Neighborhood	☐	☐	☐
Close to Employment	☐	☐	☐
Close to Shopping	☐	☐	☐
Close to Transportation	☐	☐	☐
Close to Schools / Daycare	☐	☐	☐
Close to Places of Worship	☐	☐	☐
Near Recreational Facilities	☐	☐	☐
Close to Airport	☐	☐	☐
Near Police and Fire Department	☐	☐	☐

Address ______________________ Price ______________

Bedrooms __________ Bathrooms __________ Sq.Ft. ______________

Lot Size: __________ Year Built __________ School District ______

Annual Tax __________

EXTERIOR

	Good	Average	Poor
View/Yard/Landscaping	☐	☐	☐
Trees	☐	☐	☐
Lawn (Front)	☐	☐	☐
Lawn (Back)	☐	☐	☐
Fences (condition)	☐	☐	☐
Landscaping (condition)	☐	☐	☐
Irrigation / Sprinkler	☐	☐	☐
	☐	☐	☐
House Type	☐	☐	☐
Exterior Siding	☐	☐	☐
Deck / Patio / Porch	☐	☐	☐
Garage	☐	☐	☐
Window / Doors	☐	☐	☐
Roof / Gutters	☐	☐	☐
Fencing	☐	☐	☐

HOME SYSTEMS

	Good	Average	Poor
Electrical	☐	☐	☐
Air Conditioning / Fans	☐	☐	☐
Heating	☐	☐	☐
Security	☐	☐	☐
Plumbing	☐	☐	☐
Intercom	☐	☐	☐

FEATURES

	Good	Average	Poor
Home Warranty	☐	☐	☐
Energy Saving Features	☐	☐	☐

INTERIOR

	Good	Average	Poor
Walls / Trim / Ceilings	☐	☐	☐
Flooring	☐	☐	☐
Stairs	☐	☐	☐
Storage	☐	☐	☐
Living Room	☐	☐	☐
Family Room	☐	☐	☐
Dining Room	☐	☐	☐

	Good	Average	Poor
Master Bedroom	☐	☐	☐
Bedroom 2	☐	☐	☐
Bedroom 3	☐	☐	☐
Bedroom 4	☐	☐	☐
Master Bathroom	☐	☐	☐
Bathroom 2	☐	☐	☐
Bathroom 3	☐	☐	☐
Bonus / Game Room	☐	☐	☐

	Good	Average	Poor
Kitchen	☐	☐	☐
Cabinets	☐	☐	☐
Countertop	☐	☐	☐
Counter Space	☐	☐	☐
Flooring	☐	☐	☐
Oven / Stove	☐	☐	☐
Microwave	☐	☐	☐
Layout	☐	☐	☐
Light Fixtures	☐	☐	☐
Backsplash	☐	☐	☐
Pantry	☐	☐	☐
Appliances	☐	☐	☐
Island	☐	☐	☐

	Good	Average	Poor
Basement	☐	☐	☐
Garage	☐	☐	☐

COMMUNITY

	Good	Average	Poor
Immediate Neighborhood	☐	☐	☐
Close to Employment	☐	☐	☐
Close to Shopping	☐	☐	☐
Close to Transportation	☐	☐	☐
Close to Schools / Daycare	☐	☐	☐
Close to Places of Worship	☐	☐	☐
Near Recreational Facilities	☐	☐	☐
Close to Airport	☐	☐	☐
Near Police and Fire Department	☐	☐	☐

Address ______________________ Price ____________

Bedrooms __________ Bathrooms __________ Sq.Ft. ____________

Lot Size: __________ Year Built __________ School District ________

Annual Tax __________

EXTERIOR

	Good	Average	Poor
View/Yard/Landscaping	☐	☐	☐
Trees	☐	☐	☐
Lawn (Front)	☐	☐	☐
Lawn (Back)	☐	☐	☐
Fences (condition)	☐	☐	☐
Landscaping (condition)	☐	☐	☐
Irrigation / Sprinkler	☐	☐	☐
	☐	☐	☐
House Type	☐	☐	☐
Exterior Siding	☐	☐	☐
Deck / Patio / Porch	☐	☐	☐
Garage	☐	☐	☐
Window / Doors	☐	☐	☐
Roof / Gutters	☐	☐	☐
Fencing	☐	☐	☐

HOME SYSTEMS

	Good	Average	Poor
Electrical	☐	☐	☐
Air Conditioning / Fans	☐	☐	☐
Heating	☐	☐	☐
Security	☐	☐	☐
Plumbing	☐	☐	☐
Intercom	☐	☐	☐

FEATURES

	Good	Average	Poor
Home Warranty	☐	☐	☐
Energy Saving Features	☐	☐	☐

INTERIOR

	Good	Average	Poor
Walls / Trim / Ceilings	☐	☐	☐
Flooring	☐	☐	☐
Stairs	☐	☐	☐
Storage	☐	☐	☐
Living Room	☐	☐	☐
Family Room	☐	☐	☐
Dining Room	☐	☐	☐

	Good	Average	Poor
Master Bedroom	☐	☐	☐
Bedroom 2	☐	☐	☐
Bedroom 3	☐	☐	☐
Bedroom 4	☐	☐	☐
Master Bathroom	☐	☐	☐
Bathroom 2	☐	☐	☐
Bathroom 3	☐	☐	☐
Bonus / Game Room	☐	☐	☐

	Good	Average	Poor
Kitchen	☐	☐	☐
Cabinets	☐	☐	☐
Countertop	☐	☐	☐
Counter Space	☐	☐	☐
Flooring	☐	☐	☐
Oven / Stove	☐	☐	☐
Microwave	☐	☐	☐
Layout	☐	☐	☐
Light Fixtures	☐	☐	☐
Backsplash	☐	☐	☐
Pantry	☐	☐	☐
Appliances	☐	☐	☐
Island	☐	☐	☐

	Good	Average	Poor
Basement	☐	☐	☐
Garage	☐	☐	☐

COMMUNITY

	Good	Average	Poor
Immediate Neighborhood	☐	☐	☐
Close to Employment	☐	☐	☐
Close to Shopping	☐	☐	☐
Close to Transportation	☐	☐	☐
Close to Schools / Daycare	☐	☐	☐
Close to Places of Worship	☐	☐	☐
Near Recreational Facilities	☐	☐	☐
Close to Airport	☐	☐	☐
Near Police and Fire Department	☐	☐	☐

Address ______________________ Price ____________

Bedrooms ________ Bathrooms ________ Sq.Ft. ____________

Lot Size: ________ Year Built ________ School District ______

Annual Tax ________

EXTERIOR

	Good	Average	Poor
View/Yard/Landscaping	☐	☐	☐
Trees	☐	☐	☐
Lawn (Front)	☐	☐	☐
Lawn (Back)	☐	☐	☐
Fences (condition)	☐	☐	☐
Landscaping (condition)	☐	☐	☐
Irrigation / Sprinkler	☐	☐	☐
	☐	☐	☐
House Type	☐	☐	☐
Exterior Siding	☐	☐	☐
Deck / Patio / Porch	☐	☐	☐
Garage	☐	☐	☐
Window / Doors	☐	☐	☐
Roof / Gutters	☐	☐	☐
Fencing	☐	☐	☐

HOME SYSTEMS

	Good	Average	Poor
Electrical	☐	☐	☐
Air Conditioning / Fans	☐	☐	☐
Heating	☐	☐	☐
Security	☐	☐	☐
Plumbing	☐	☐	☐
Intercom	☐	☐	☐

FEATURES

	Good	Average	Poor
Home Warranty	☐	☐	☐
Energy Saving Features	☐	☐	☐

INTERIOR

	Good	Average	Poor
Walls / Trim / Ceilings	☐	☐	☐
Flooring	☐	☐	☐
Stairs	☐	☐	☐
Storage	☐	☐	☐
Living Room	☐	☐	☐
Family Room	☐	☐	☐
Dining Room	☐	☐	☐

	Good	Average	Poor
Master Bedroom	☐	☐	☐
Bedroom 2	☐	☐	☐
Bedroom 3	☐	☐	☐
Bedroom 4	☐	☐	☐
Master Bathroom	☐	☐	☐
Bathroom 2	☐	☐	☐
Bathroom 3	☐	☐	☐
Bonus / Game Room	☐	☐	☐

	Good	Average	Poor
Kitchen	☐	☐	☐
Cabinets	☐	☐	☐
Countertop	☐	☐	☐
Counter Space	☐	☐	☐
Flooring	☐	☐	☐
Oven / Stove	☐	☐	☐
Microwave	☐	☐	☐
Layout	☐	☐	☐
Light Fixtures	☐	☐	☐
Backsplash	☐	☐	☐
Pantry	☐	☐	☐
Appliances	☐	☐	☐
Island	☐	☐	☐

	Good	Average	Poor
Basement	☐	☐	☐
Garage	☐	☐	☐

COMMUNITY

	Good	Average	Poor
Immediate Neighborhood	☐	☐	☐
Close to Employment	☐	☐	☐
Close to Shopping	☐	☐	☐
Close to Transportation	☐	☐	☐
Close to Schools / Daycare	☐	☐	☐
Close to Places of Worship	☐	☐	☐
Near Recreational Facilities	☐	☐	☐
Close to Airport	☐	☐	☐
Near Police and Fire Department	☐	☐	☐

Address ______________________ Price ______________

Bedrooms ______________ Bathrooms ______________ Sq.Ft. ______________

Lot Size: ______________ Year Built ______________ School District ______________

Annual Tax ______________

EXTERIOR

	Good	Average	Poor
View/Yard/Landscaping	☐	☐	☐
Trees	☐	☐	☐
Lawn (Front)	☐	☐	☐
Lawn (Back)	☐	☐	☐
Fences (condition)	☐	☐	☐
Landscaping (condition)	☐	☐	☐
Irrigation / Sprinkler	☐	☐	☐
	☐	☐	☐
House Type	☐	☐	☐
Exterior Siding	☐	☐	☐
Deck / Patio / Porch	☐	☐	☐
Garage	☐	☐	☐
Window / Doors	☐	☐	☐
Roof / Gutters	☐	☐	☐
Fencing	☐	☐	☐

HOME SYSTEMS

	Good	Average	Poor
Electrical	☐	☐	☐
Air Conditioning / Fans	☐	☐	☐
Heating	☐	☐	☐
Security	☐	☐	☐
Plumbing	☐	☐	☐
Intercom	☐	☐	☐

FEATURES

	Good	Average	Poor
Home Warranty	☐	☐	☐
Energy Saving Features	☐	☐	☐

INTERIOR

	Good	Average	Poor
Walls / Trim / Ceilings	☐	☐	☐
Flooring	☐	☐	☐
Stairs	☐	☐	☐
Storage	☐	☐	☐
Living Room	☐	☐	☐
Family Room	☐	☐	☐
Dining Room	☐	☐	☐

	Good	Average	Poor
Master Bedroom	☐	☐	☐
Bedroom 2	☐	☐	☐
Bedroom 3	☐	☐	☐
Bedroom 4	☐	☐	☐
Master Bathroom	☐	☐	☐
Bathroom 2	☐	☐	☐
Bathroom 3	☐	☐	☐
Bonus / Game Room	☐	☐	☐

	Good	Average	Poor
Kitchen	☐	☐	☐
Cabinets	☐	☐	☐
Countertop	☐	☐	☐
Counter Space	☐	☐	☐
Flooring	☐	☐	☐
Oven / Stove	☐	☐	☐
Microwave	☐	☐	☐
Layout	☐	☐	☐
Light Fixtures	☐	☐	☐
Backsplash	☐	☐	☐
Pantry	☐	☐	☐
Appliances	☐	☐	☐
Island	☐	☐	☐

	Good	Average	Poor
Basement	☐	☐	☐
Garage	☐	☐	☐

COMMUNITY

	Good	Average	Poor
Immediate Neighborhood	☐	☐	☐
Close to Employment	☐	☐	☐
Close to Shopping	☐	☐	☐
Close to Transportation	☐	☐	☐
Close to Schools / Daycare	☐	☐	☐
Close to Places of Worship	☐	☐	☐
Near Recreational Facilities	☐	☐	☐
Close to Airport	☐	☐	☐
Near Police and Fire Department	☐	☐	☐

Address ______________________ Price ____________

Bedrooms ____________ Bathrooms ____________ Sq.Ft. ____________

Lot Size: ____________ Year Built ____________ School District ________

Annual Tax ____________

EXTERIOR

	Good	Average	Poor
View/Yard/Landscaping	☐	☐	☐
Trees	☐	☐	☐
Lawn (Front)	☐	☐	☐
Lawn (Back)	☐	☐	☐
Fences (condition)	☐	☐	☐
Landscaping (condition)	☐	☐	☐
Irrigation / Sprinkler	☐	☐	☐
	☐	☐	☐
House Type	☐	☐	☐
Exterior Siding	☐	☐	☐
Deck / Patio / Porch	☐	☐	☐
Garage	☐	☐	☐
Window / Doors	☐	☐	☐
Roof / Gutters	☐	☐	☐
Fencing	☐	☐	☐

HOME SYSTEMS

	Good	Average	Poor
Electrical	☐	☐	☐
Air Conditioning / Fans	☐	☐	☐
Heating	☐	☐	☐
Security	☐	☐	☐
Plumbing	☐	☐	☐
Intercom	☐	☐	☐

FEATURES

	Good	Average	Poor
Home Warranty	☐	☐	☐
Energy Saving Features	☐	☐	☐

INTERIOR

	Good	Average	Poor
Walls / Trim / Ceilings	☐	☐	☐
Flooring	☐	☐	☐
Stairs	☐	☐	☐
Storage	☐	☐	☐
Living Room	☐	☐	☐
Family Room	☐	☐	☐
Dining Room	☐	☐	☐

	Good	Average	Poor
Master Bedroom	☐	☐	☐
Bedroom 2	☐	☐	☐
Bedroom 3	☐	☐	☐
Bedroom 4	☐	☐	☐
Master Bathroom	☐	☐	☐
Bathroom 2	☐	☐	☐
Bathroom 3	☐	☐	☐
Bonus / Game Room	☐	☐	☐

	Good	Average	Poor
Kitchen	☐	☐	☐
Cabinets	☐	☐	☐
Countertop	☐	☐	☐
Counter Space	☐	☐	☐
Flooring	☐	☐	☐
Oven / Stove	☐	☐	☐
Microwave	☐	☐	☐
Layout	☐	☐	☐
Light Fixtures	☐	☐	☐
Backsplash	☐	☐	☐
Pantry	☐	☐	☐
Appliances	☐	☐	☐
Island	☐	☐	☐

	Good	Average	Poor
Basement	☐	☐	☐
Garage	☐	☐	☐

COMMUNITY

	Good	Average	Poor
Immediate Neighborhood	☐	☐	☐
Close to Employment	☐	☐	☐
Close to Shopping	☐	☐	☐
Close to Transportation	☐	☐	☐
Close to Schools / Daycare	☐	☐	☐
Close to Places of Worship	☐	☐	☐
Near Recreational Facilities	☐	☐	☐
Close to Airport	☐	☐	☐
Near Police and Fire Department	☐	☐	☐

Address ____________________ Price ____________

Bedrooms ________ Bathrooms ________ Sq.Ft. ____________

Lot Size: ________ Year Built ________ School District ______

Annual Tax ________

EXTERIOR

	Good	Average	Poor
View/Yard/Landscaping	☐	☐	☐
Trees	☐	☐	☐
Lawn (Front)	☐	☐	☐
Lawn (Back)	☐	☐	☐
Fences (condition)	☐	☐	☐
Landscaping (condition)	☐	☐	☐
Irrigation / Sprinkler	☐	☐	☐
	☐	☐	☐
House Type	☐	☐	☐
Exterior Siding	☐	☐	☐
Deck / Patio / Porch	☐	☐	☐
Garage	☐	☐	☐
Window / Doors	☐	☐	☐
Roof / Gutters	☐	☐	☐
Fencing	☐	☐	☐

HOME SYSTEMS

	Good	Average	Poor
Electrical	☐	☐	☐
Air Conditioning / Fans	☐	☐	☐
Heating	☐	☐	☐
Security	☐	☐	☐
Plumbing	☐	☐	☐
Intercom	☐	☐	☐

FEATURES

	Good	Average	Poor
Home Warranty	☐	☐	☐
Energy Saving Features	☐	☐	☐

INTERIOR

	Good	Average	Poor
Walls / Trim / Ceilings	☐	☐	☐
Flooring	☐	☐	☐
Stairs	☐	☐	☐
Storage	☐	☐	☐
Living Room	☐	☐	☐
Family Room	☐	☐	☐
Dining Room	☐	☐	☐

	Good	Average	Poor
Master Bedroom	☐	☐	☐
Bedroom 2	☐	☐	☐
Bedroom 3	☐	☐	☐
Bedroom 4	☐	☐	☐
Master Bathroom	☐	☐	☐
Bathroom 2	☐	☐	☐
Bathroom 3	☐	☐	☐
Bonus / Game Room	☐	☐	☐

	Good	Average	Poor
Kitchen	☐	☐	☐
Cabinets	☐	☐	☐
Countertop	☐	☐	☐
Counter Space	☐	☐	☐
Flooring	☐	☐	☐
Oven / Stove	☐	☐	☐
Microwave	☐	☐	☐
Layout	☐	☐	☐
Light Fixtures	☐	☐	☐
Backsplash	☐	☐	☐
Pantry	☐	☐	☐
Appliances	☐	☐	☐
Island	☐	☐	☐

	Good	Average	Poor
Basement	☐	☐	☐
Garage	☐	☐	☐

COMMUNITY

	Good	Average	Poor
Immediate Neighborhood	☐	☐	☐
Close to Employment	☐	☐	☐
Close to Shopping	☐	☐	☐
Close to Transportation	☐	☐	☐
Close to Schools / Daycare	☐	☐	☐
Close to Places of Worship	☐	☐	☐
Near Recreational Facilities	☐	☐	☐
Close to Airport	☐	☐	☐
Near Police and Fire Department	☐	☐	☐

Address ______________________ Price ______________

Bedrooms __________ Bathrooms __________ Sq.Ft. ______________

Lot Size: __________ Year Built __________ School District __________

Annual Tax __________

EXTERIOR

	Good	Average	Poor
View/Yard/Landscaping	☐	☐	☐
Trees	☐	☐	☐
Lawn (Front)	☐	☐	☐
Lawn (Back)	☐	☐	☐
Fences (condition)	☐	☐	☐
Landscaping (condition)	☐	☐	☐
Irrigation / Sprinkler	☐	☐	☐
	☐	☐	☐
House Type	☐	☐	☐
Exterior Siding	☐	☐	☐
Deck / Patio / Porch	☐	☐	☐
Garage	☐	☐	☐
Window / Doors	☐	☐	☐
Roof / Gutters	☐	☐	☐
Fencing	☐	☐	☐

HOME SYSTEMS

	Good	Average	Poor
Electrical	☐	☐	☐
Air Conditioning / Fans	☐	☐	☐
Heating	☐	☐	☐
Security	☐	☐	☐
Plumbing	☐	☐	☐
Intercom	☐	☐	☐

FEATURES

	Good	Average	Poor
Home Warranty	☐	☐	☐
Energy Saving Features	☐	☐	☐

INTERIOR

	Good	Average	Poor
Walls / Trim / Ceilings	☐	☐	☐
Flooring	☐	☐	☐
Stairs	☐	☐	☐
Storage	☐	☐	☐
Living Room	☐	☐	☐
Family Room	☐	☐	☐
Dining Room	☐	☐	☐

	Good	Average	Poor
Master Bedroom	☐	☐	☐
Bedroom 2	☐	☐	☐
Bedroom 3	☐	☐	☐
Bedroom 4	☐	☐	☐
Master Bathroom	☐	☐	☐
Bathroom 2	☐	☐	☐
Bathroom 3	☐	☐	☐
Bonus / Game Room	☐	☐	☐

	Good	Average	Poor
Kitchen	☐	☐	☐
Cabinets	☐	☐	☐
Countertop	☐	☐	☐
Counter Space	☐	☐	☐
Flooring	☐	☐	☐
Oven / Stove	☐	☐	☐
Microwave	☐	☐	☐
Layout	☐	☐	☐
Light Fixtures	☐	☐	☐
Backsplash	☐	☐	☐
Pantry	☐	☐	☐
Appliances	☐	☐	☐
Island	☐	☐	☐

	Good	Average	Poor
Basement	☐	☐	☐
Garage	☐	☐	☐

COMMUNITY

	Good	Average	Poor
Immediate Neighborhood	☐	☐	☐
Close to Employment	☐	☐	☐
Close to Shopping	☐	☐	☐
Close to Transportation	☐	☐	☐
Close to Schools / Daycare	☐	☐	☐
Close to Places of Worship	☐	☐	☐
Near Recreational Facilities	☐	☐	☐
Close to Airport	☐	☐	☐
Near Police and Fire Department	☐	☐	☐

Address ______________________________ Price ______________

Bedrooms __________ Bathrooms ___________ Sq.Ft. ______________

Lot Size: __________ Year Built ___________ School District ________

Annual Tax _________

EXTERIOR

	Good	Average	Poor
View/Yard/Landscaping	☐	☐	☐
Trees	☐	☐	☐
Lawn (Front)	☐	☐	☐
Lawn (Back)	☐	☐	☐
Fences (condition)	☐	☐	☐
Landscaping (condition)	☐	☐	☐
Irrigation / Sprinkler	☐	☐	☐
	☐	☐	☐
House Type	☐	☐	☐
Exterior Siding	☐	☐	☐
Deck / Patio / Porch	☐	☐	☐
Garage	☐	☐	☐
Window / Doors	☐	☐	☐
Roof / Gutters	☐	☐	☐
Fencing	☐	☐	☐

HOME SYSTEMS

	Good	Average	Poor
Electrical	☐	☐	☐
Air Conditioning / Fans	☐	☐	☐
Heating	☐	☐	☐
Security	☐	☐	☐
Plumbing	☐	☐	☐
Intercom	☐	☐	☐

FEATURES

	Good	Average	Poor
Home Warranty	☐	☐	☐
Energy Saving Features	☐	☐	☐

INTERIOR

	Good	Average	Poor
Walls / Trim / Ceilings	☐	☐	☐
Flooring	☐	☐	☐
Stairs	☐	☐	☐
Storage	☐	☐	☐
Living Room	☐	☐	☐
Family Room	☐	☐	☐
Dining Room	☐	☐	☐

	Good	Average	Poor
Master Bedroom	☐	☐	☐
Bedroom 2	☐	☐	☐
Bedroom 3	☐	☐	☐
Bedroom 4	☐	☐	☐
Master Bathroom	☐	☐	☐
Bathroom 2	☐	☐	☐
Bathroom 3	☐	☐	☐
Bonus / Game Room	☐	☐	☐

	Good	Average	Poor
Kitchen	☐	☐	☐
Cabinets	☐	☐	☐
Countertop	☐	☐	☐
Counter Space	☐	☐	☐
Flooring	☐	☐	☐
Oven / Stove	☐	☐	☐
Microwave	☐	☐	☐
Layout	☐	☐	☐
Light Fixtures	☐	☐	☐
Backsplash	☐	☐	☐
Pantry	☐	☐	☐
Appliances	☐	☐	☐
Island	☐	☐	☐

	Good	Average	Poor
Basement	☐	☐	☐
Garage	☐	☐	☐

COMMUNITY

	Good	Average	Poor
Immediate Neighborhood	☐	☐	☐
Close to Employment	☐	☐	☐
Close to Shopping	☐	☐	☐
Close to Transportation	☐	☐	☐
Close to Schools / Daycare	☐	☐	☐
Close to Places of Worship	☐	☐	☐
Near Recreational Facilities	☐	☐	☐
Close to Airport	☐	☐	☐
Near Police and Fire Department	☐	☐	☐

Address ____________________ Price ____________

Bedrooms __________ Bathrooms __________ Sq.Ft. ____________

Lot Size: __________ Year Built __________ School District ________

Annual Tax __________

EXTERIOR

	Good	Average	Poor
View/Yard/Landscaping	☐	☐	☐
Trees	☐	☐	☐
Lawn (Front)	☐	☐	☐
Lawn (Back)	☐	☐	☐
Fences (condition)	☐	☐	☐
Landscaping (condition)	☐	☐	☐
Irrigation / Sprinkler	☐	☐	☐
	☐	☐	☐
House Type	☐	☐	☐
Exterior Siding	☐	☐	☐
Deck / Patio / Porch	☐	☐	☐
Garage	☐	☐	☐
Window / Doors	☐	☐	☐
Roof / Gutters	☐	☐	☐
Fencing	☐	☐	☐

HOME SYSTEMS

	Good	Average	Poor
Electrical	☐	☐	☐
Air Conditioning / Fans	☐	☐	☐
Heating	☐	☐	☐
Security	☐	☐	☐
Plumbing	☐	☐	☐
Intercom	☐	☐	☐

FEATURES

	Good	Average	Poor
Home Warranty	☐	☐	☐
Energy Saving Features	☐	☐	☐

INTERIOR

	Good	Average	Poor
Walls / Trim / Ceilings	☐	☐	☐
Flooring	☐	☐	☐
Stairs	☐	☐	☐
Storage	☐	☐	☐
Living Room	☐	☐	☐
Family Room	☐	☐	☐
Dining Room	☐	☐	☐

	Good	Average	Poor
Master Bedroom	☐	☐	☐
Bedroom 2	☐	☐	☐
Bedroom 3	☐	☐	☐
Bedroom 4	☐	☐	☐
Master Bathroom	☐	☐	☐
Bathroom 2	☐	☐	☐
Bathroom 3	☐	☐	☐
Bonus / Game Room	☐	☐	☐

	Good	Average	Poor
Kitchen	☐	☐	☐
Cabinets	☐	☐	☐
Countertop	☐	☐	☐
Counter Space	☐	☐	☐
Flooring	☐	☐	☐
Oven / Stove	☐	☐	☐
Microwave	☐	☐	☐
Layout	☐	☐	☐
Light Fixtures	☐	☐	☐
Backsplash	☐	☐	☐
Pantry	☐	☐	☐
Appliances	☐	☐	☐
Island	☐	☐	☐

	Good	Average	Poor
Basement	☐	☐	☐
Garage	☐	☐	☐

COMMUNITY

	Good	Average	Poor
Immediate Neighborhood	☐	☐	☐
Close to Employment	☐	☐	☐
Close to Shopping	☐	☐	☐
Close to Transportation	☐	☐	☐
Close to Schools / Daycare	☐	☐	☐
Close to Places of Worship	☐	☐	☐
Near Recreational Facilities	☐	☐	☐
Close to Airport	☐	☐	☐
Near Police and Fire Department	☐	☐	☐

Address ______________________ Price ____________

Bedrooms ________ Bathrooms ________ Sq.Ft. ____________

Lot Size: ________ Year Built ________ School District ______

Annual Tax ________

EXTERIOR

	Good	Average	Poor
View/Yard/Landscaping	☐	☐	☐
Trees	☐	☐	☐
Lawn (Front)	☐	☐	☐
Lawn (Back)	☐	☐	☐
Fences (condition)	☐	☐	☐
Landscaping (condition)	☐	☐	☐
Irrigation / Sprinkler	☐	☐	☐
	☐	☐	☐
House Type	☐	☐	☐
Exterior Siding	☐	☐	☐
Deck / Patio / Porch	☐	☐	☐
Garage	☐	☐	☐
Window / Doors	☐	☐	☐
Roof / Gutters	☐	☐	☐
Fencing	☐	☐	☐

HOME SYSTEMS

	Good	Average	Poor
Electrical	☐	☐	☐
Air Conditioning / Fans	☐	☐	☐
Heating	☐	☐	☐
Security	☐	☐	☐
Plumbing	☐	☐	☐
Intercom	☐	☐	☐

FEATURES

	Good	Average	Poor
Home Warranty	☐	☐	☐
Energy Saving Features	☐	☐	☐

INTERIOR

	Good	Average	Poor
Walls / Trim / Ceilings	☐	☐	☐
Flooring	☐	☐	☐
Stairs	☐	☐	☐
Storage	☐	☐	☐
Living Room	☐	☐	☐
Family Room	☐	☐	☐
Dining Room	☐	☐	☐

	Good	Average	Poor
Master Bedroom	☐	☐	☐
Bedroom 2	☐	☐	☐
Bedroom 3	☐	☐	☐
Bedroom 4	☐	☐	☐
Master Bathroom	☐	☐	☐
Bathroom 2	☐	☐	☐
Bathroom 3	☐	☐	☐
Bonus / Game Room	☐	☐	☐

	Good	Average	Poor
Kitchen	☐	☐	☐
Cabinets	☐	☐	☐
Countertop	☐	☐	☐
Counter Space	☐	☐	☐
Flooring	☐	☐	☐
Oven / Stove	☐	☐	☐
Microwave	☐	☐	☐
Layout	☐	☐	☐
Light Fixtures	☐	☐	☐
Backsplash	☐	☐	☐
Pantry	☐	☐	☐
Appliances	☐	☐	☐
Island	☐	☐	☐

	Good	Average	Poor
Basement	☐	☐	☐
Garage	☐	☐	☐

COMMUNITY

	Good	Average	Poor
Immediate Neighborhood	☐	☐	☐
Close to Employment	☐	☐	☐
Close to Shopping	☐	☐	☐
Close to Transportation	☐	☐	☐
Close to Schools / Daycare	☐	☐	☐
Close to Places of Worship	☐	☐	☐
Near Recreational Facilities	☐	☐	☐
Close to Airport	☐	☐	☐
Near Police and Fire Department	☐	☐	☐

Address ____________________ Price ____________

Bedrooms ________ Bathrooms ________ Sq.Ft. ____________

Lot Size: ________ Year Built ________ School District ________

Annual Tax ________

EXTERIOR

	Good	Average	Poor
View/Yard/Landscaping	☐	☐	☐
Trees	☐	☐	☐
Lawn (Front)	☐	☐	☐
Lawn (Back)	☐	☐	☐
Fences (condition)	☐	☐	☐
Landscaping (condition)	☐	☐	☐
Irrigation / Sprinkler	☐	☐	☐
	☐	☐	☐
House Type	☐	☐	☐
Exterior Siding	☐	☐	☐
Deck / Patio / Porch	☐	☐	☐
Garage	☐	☐	☐
Window / Doors	☐	☐	☐
Roof / Gutters	☐	☐	☐
Fencing	☐	☐	☐

HOME SYSTEMS

	Good	Average	Poor
Electrical	☐	☐	☐
Air Conditioning / Fans	☐	☐	☐
Heating	☐	☐	☐
Security	☐	☐	☐
Plumbing	☐	☐	☐
Intercom	☐	☐	☐

FEATURES

	Good	Average	Poor
Home Warranty	☐	☐	☐
Energy Saving Features	☐	☐	☐

INTERIOR

	Good	Average	Poor
Walls / Trim / Ceilings	☐	☐	☐
Flooring	☐	☐	☐
Stairs	☐	☐	☐
Storage	☐	☐	☐
Living Room	☐	☐	☐
Family Room	☐	☐	☐
Dining Room	☐	☐	☐

	Good	Average	Poor
Master Bedroom	☐	☐	☐
Bedroom 2	☐	☐	☐
Bedroom 3	☐	☐	☐
Bedroom 4	☐	☐	☐
Master Bathroom	☐	☐	☐
Bathroom 2	☐	☐	☐
Bathroom 3	☐	☐	☐
Bonus / Game Room	☐	☐	☐

	Good	Average	Poor
Kitchen	☐	☐	☐
Cabinets	☐	☐	☐
Countertop	☐	☐	☐
Counter Space	☐	☐	☐
Flooring	☐	☐	☐
Oven / Stove	☐	☐	☐
Microwave	☐	☐	☐
Layout	☐	☐	☐
Light Fixtures	☐	☐	☐
Backsplash	☐	☐	☐
Pantry	☐	☐	☐
Appliances	☐	☐	☐
Island	☐	☐	☐

	Good	Average	Poor
Basement	☐	☐	☐
Garage	☐	☐	☐

COMMUNITY

	Good	Average	Poor
Immediate Neighborhood	☐	☐	☐
Close to Employment	☐	☐	☐
Close to Shopping	☐	☐	☐
Close to Transportation	☐	☐	☐
Close to Schools / Daycare	☐	☐	☐
Close to Places of Worship	☐	☐	☐
Near Recreational Facilities	☐	☐	☐
Close to Airport	☐	☐	☐
Near Police and Fire Department	☐	☐	☐

Address ______________________ Price __________

Bedrooms ________ Bathrooms ________ Sq.Ft. __________

Lot Size: ________ Year Built ________ School District ________

Annual Tax ________

EXTERIOR

	Good	Average	Poor
View/Yard/Landscaping	☐	☐	☐
Trees	☐	☐	☐
Lawn (Front)	☐	☐	☐
Lawn (Back)	☐	☐	☐
Fences (condition)	☐	☐	☐
Landscaping (condition)	☐	☐	☐
Irrigation / Sprinkler	☐	☐	☐
	☐	☐	☐
House Type	☐	☐	☐
Exterior Siding	☐	☐	☐
Deck / Patio / Porch	☐	☐	☐
Garage	☐	☐	☐
Window / Doors	☐	☐	☐
Roof / Gutters	☐	☐	☐
Fencing	☐	☐	☐

HOME SYSTEMS

	Good	Average	Poor
Electrical	☐	☐	☐
Air Conditioning / Fans	☐	☐	☐
Heating	☐	☐	☐
Security	☐	☐	☐
Plumbing	☐	☐	☐
Intercom	☐	☐	☐

FEATURES

	Good	Average	Poor
Home Warranty	☐	☐	☐
Energy Saving Features	☐	☐	☐

INTERIOR

	Good	Average	Poor
Walls / Trim / Ceilings	☐	☐	☐
Flooring	☐	☐	☐
Stairs	☐	☐	☐
Storage	☐	☐	☐
Living Room	☐	☐	☐
Family Room	☐	☐	☐
Dining Room	☐	☐	☐

	Good	Average	Poor
Master Bedroom	☐	☐	☐
Bedroom 2	☐	☐	☐
Bedroom 3	☐	☐	☐
Bedroom 4	☐	☐	☐
Master Bathroom	☐	☐	☐
Bathroom 2	☐	☐	☐
Bathroom 3	☐	☐	☐
Bonus / Game Room	☐	☐	☐

	Good	Average	Poor
Kitchen	☐	☐	☐
Cabinets	☐	☐	☐
Countertop	☐	☐	☐
Counter Space	☐	☐	☐
Flooring	☐	☐	☐
Oven / Stove	☐	☐	☐
Microwave	☐	☐	☐
Layout	☐	☐	☐
Light Fixtures	☐	☐	☐
Backsplash	☐	☐	☐
Pantry	☐	☐	☐
Appliances	☐	☐	☐
Island	☐	☐	☐

	Good	Average	Poor
Basement	☐	☐	☐
Garage	☐	☐	☐

COMMUNITY

	Good	Average	Poor
Immediate Neighborhood	☐	☐	☐
Close to Employment	☐	☐	☐
Close to Shopping	☐	☐	☐
Close to Transportation	☐	☐	☐
Close to Schools / Daycare	☐	☐	☐
Close to Places of Worship	☐	☐	☐
Near Recreational Facilities	☐	☐	☐
Close to Airport	☐	☐	☐
Near Police and Fire Department	☐	☐	☐

Address ______________________ Price ____________

Bedrooms ________ Bathrooms ________ Sq.Ft. ____________

Lot Size: ________ Year Built ________ School District ______

Annual Tax ________

EXTERIOR

	Good	Average	Poor
View/Yard/Landscaping	☐	☐	☐
Trees	☐	☐	☐
Lawn (Front)	☐	☐	☐
Lawn (Back)	☐	☐	☐
Fences (condition)	☐	☐	☐
Landscaping (condition)	☐	☐	☐
Irrigation / Sprinkler	☐	☐	☐
	☐	☐	☐
House Type	☐	☐	☐
Exterior Siding	☐	☐	☐
Deck / Patio / Porch	☐	☐	☐
Garage	☐	☐	☐
Window / Doors	☐	☐	☐
Roof / Gutters	☐	☐	☐
Fencing	☐	☐	☐

HOME SYSTEMS

	Good	Average	Poor
Electrical	☐	☐	☐
Air Conditioning / Fans	☐	☐	☐
Heating	☐	☐	☐
Security	☐	☐	☐
Plumbing	☐	☐	☐
Intercom	☐	☐	☐

FEATURES

	Good	Average	Poor
Home Warranty	☐	☐	☐
Energy Saving Features	☐	☐	☐

INTERIOR

	Good	Average	Poor
Walls / Trim / Ceilings	☐	☐	☐
Flooring	☐	☐	☐
Stairs	☐	☐	☐
Storage	☐	☐	☐
Living Room	☐	☐	☐
Family Room	☐	☐	☐
Dining Room	☐	☐	☐

	Good	Average	Poor
Master Bedroom	☐	☐	☐
Bedroom 2	☐	☐	☐
Bedroom 3	☐	☐	☐
Bedroom 4	☐	☐	☐
Master Bathroom	☐	☐	☐
Bathroom 2	☐	☐	☐
Bathroom 3	☐	☐	☐
Bonus / Game Room	☐	☐	☐

	Good	Average	Poor
Kitchen	☐	☐	☐
Cabinets	☐	☐	☐
Countertop	☐	☐	☐
Counter Space	☐	☐	☐
Flooring	☐	☐	☐
Oven / Stove	☐	☐	☐
Microwave	☐	☐	☐
Layout	☐	☐	☐
Light Fixtures	☐	☐	☐
Backsplash	☐	☐	☐
Pantry	☐	☐	☐
Appliances	☐	☐	☐
Island	☐	☐	☐

	Good	Average	Poor
Basement	☐	☐	☐
Garage	☐	☐	☐

COMMUNITY

	Good	Average	Poor
Immediate Neighborhood	☐	☐	☐
Close to Employment	☐	☐	☐
Close to Shopping	☐	☐	☐
Close to Transportation	☐	☐	☐
Close to Schools / Daycare	☐	☐	☐
Close to Places of Worship	☐	☐	☐
Near Recreational Facilities	☐	☐	☐
Close to Airport	☐	☐	☐
Near Police and Fire Department	☐	☐	☐

Address ______________________ Price ______________

Bedrooms ____________ Bathrooms ____________ Sq.Ft. ______________

Lot Size: ____________ Year Built ____________ School District ________

Annual Tax ____________

EXTERIOR

	Good	Average	Poor
View/Yard/Landscaping	☐	☐	☐
Trees	☐	☐	☐
Lawn (Front)	☐	☐	☐
Lawn (Back)	☐	☐	☐
Fences (condition)	☐	☐	☐
Landscaping (condition)	☐	☐	☐
Irrigation / Sprinkler	☐	☐	☐
	☐	☐	☐
House Type	☐	☐	☐
Exterior Siding	☐	☐	☐
Deck / Patio / Porch	☐	☐	☐
Garage	☐	☐	☐
Window / Doors	☐	☐	☐
Roof / Gutters	☐	☐	☐
Fencing	☐	☐	☐

HOME SYSTEMS

	Good	Average	Poor
Electrical	☐	☐	☐
Air Conditioning / Fans	☐	☐	☐
Heating	☐	☐	☐
Security	☐	☐	☐
Plumbing	☐	☐	☐
Intercom	☐	☐	☐

FEATURES

	Good	Average	Poor
Home Warranty	☐	☐	☐
Energy Saving Features	☐	☐	☐

INTERIOR

	Good	Average	Poor
Walls / Trim / Ceilings	☐	☐	☐
Flooring	☐	☐	☐
Stairs	☐	☐	☐
Storage	☐	☐	☐
Living Room	☐	☐	☐
Family Room	☐	☐	☐
Dining Room	☐	☐	☐

	Good	Average	Poor
Master Bedroom	☐	☐	☐
Bedroom 2	☐	☐	☐
Bedroom 3	☐	☐	☐
Bedroom 4	☐	☐	☐
Master Bathroom	☐	☐	☐
Bathroom 2	☐	☐	☐
Bathroom 3	☐	☐	☐
Bonus / Game Room	☐	☐	☐

	Good	Average	Poor
Kitchen	☐	☐	☐
Cabinets	☐	☐	☐
Countertop	☐	☐	☐
Counter Space	☐	☐	☐
Flooring	☐	☐	☐
Oven / Stove	☐	☐	☐
Microwave	☐	☐	☐
Layout	☐	☐	☐
Light Fixtures	☐	☐	☐
Backsplash	☐	☐	☐
Pantry	☐	☐	☐
Appliances	☐	☐	☐
Island	☐	☐	☐

	Good	Average	Poor
Basement	☐	☐	☐
Garage	☐	☐	☐

COMMUNITY

	Good	Average	Poor
Immediate Neighborhood	☐	☐	☐
Close to Employment	☐	☐	☐
Close to Shopping	☐	☐	☐
Close to Transportation	☐	☐	☐
Close to Schools / Daycare	☐	☐	☐
Close to Places of Worship	☐	☐	☐
Near Recreational Facilities	☐	☐	☐
Close to Airport	☐	☐	☐
Near Police and Fire Department	☐	☐	☐

Address ______________________________ Price ______________

Bedrooms __________ Bathrooms __________ Sq.Ft. ______________

Lot Size: __________ Year Built __________ School District _______

Annual Tax __________

EXTERIOR

	Good	Average	Poor
View/Yard/Landscaping	☐	☐	☐
Trees	☐	☐	☐
Lawn (Front)	☐	☐	☐
Lawn (Back)	☐	☐	☐
Fences (condition)	☐	☐	☐
Landscaping (condition)	☐	☐	☐
Irrigation / Sprinkler	☐	☐	☐
	☐	☐	☐
House Type	☐	☐	☐
Exterior Siding	☐	☐	☐
Deck / Patio / Porch	☐	☐	☐
Garage	☐	☐	☐
Window / Doors	☐	☐	☐
Roof / Gutters	☐	☐	☐
Fencing	☐	☐	☐

HOME SYSTEMS

	Good	Average	Poor
Electrical	☐	☐	☐
Air Conditioning / Fans	☐	☐	☐
Heating	☐	☐	☐
Security	☐	☐	☐
Plumbing	☐	☐	☐
Intercom	☐	☐	☐

FEATURES

	Good	Average	Poor
Home Warranty	☐	☐	☐
Energy Saving Features	☐	☐	☐

INTERIOR

	Good	Average	Poor
Walls / Trim / Ceilings	☐	☐	☐
Flooring	☐	☐	☐
Stairs	☐	☐	☐
Storage	☐	☐	☐
Living Room	☐	☐	☐
Family Room	☐	☐	☐
Dining Room	☐	☐	☐

	Good	Average	Poor
Master Bedroom	☐	☐	☐
Bedroom 2	☐	☐	☐
Bedroom 3	☐	☐	☐
Bedroom 4	☐	☐	☐
Master Bathroom	☐	☐	☐
Bathroom 2	☐	☐	☐
Bathroom 3	☐	☐	☐
Bonus / Game Room	☐	☐	☐

	Good	Average	Poor
Kitchen	☐	☐	☐
Cabinets	☐	☐	☐
Countertop	☐	☐	☐
Counter Space	☐	☐	☐
Flooring	☐	☐	☐
Oven / Stove	☐	☐	☐
Microwave	☐	☐	☐
Layout	☐	☐	☐
Light Fixtures	☐	☐	☐
Backsplash	☐	☐	☐
Pantry	☐	☐	☐
Appliances	☐	☐	☐
Island	☐	☐	☐

	Good	Average	Poor
Basement	☐	☐	☐
Garage	☐	☐	☐

COMMUNITY

	Good	Average	Poor
Immediate Neighborhood	☐	☐	☐
Close to Employment	☐	☐	☐
Close to Shopping	☐	☐	☐
Close to Transportation	☐	☐	☐
Close to Schools / Daycare	☐	☐	☐
Close to Places of Worship	☐	☐	☐
Near Recreational Facilities	☐	☐	☐
Close to Airport	☐	☐	☐
Near Police and Fire Department	☐	☐	☐

Address ______________________ Price ______________

Bedrooms ________ Bathrooms ________ Sq.Ft. ______________

Lot Size: ________ Year Built ________ School District ________

Annual Tax ________

EXTERIOR

	Good	Average	Poor
View/Yard/Landscaping	☐	☐	☐
Trees	☐	☐	☐
Lawn (Front)	☐	☐	☐
Lawn (Back)	☐	☐	☐
Fences (condition)	☐	☐	☐
Landscaping (condition)	☐	☐	☐
Irrigation / Sprinkler	☐	☐	☐
	☐	☐	☐
House Type	☐	☐	☐
Exterior Siding	☐	☐	☐
Deck / Patio / Porch	☐	☐	☐
Garage	☐	☐	☐
Window / Doors	☐	☐	☐
Roof / Gutters	☐	☐	☐
Fencing	☐	☐	☐

HOME SYSTEMS

	Good	Average	Poor
Electrical	☐	☐	☐
Air Conditioning / Fans	☐	☐	☐
Heating	☐	☐	☐
Security	☐	☐	☐
Plumbing	☐	☐	☐
Intercom	☐	☐	☐

FEATURES

	Good	Average	Poor
Home Warranty	☐	☐	☐
Energy Saving Features	☐	☐	☐

INTERIOR

	Good	Average	Poor
Walls / Trim / Ceilings	☐	☐	☐
Flooring	☐	☐	☐
Stairs	☐	☐	☐
Storage	☐	☐	☐
Living Room	☐	☐	☐
Family Room	☐	☐	☐
Dining Room	☐	☐	☐

	Good	Average	Poor
Master Bedroom	☐	☐	☐
Bedroom 2	☐	☐	☐
Bedroom 3	☐	☐	☐
Bedroom 4	☐	☐	☐
Master Bathroom	☐	☐	☐
Bathroom 2	☐	☐	☐
Bathroom 3	☐	☐	☐
Bonus / Game Room	☐	☐	☐

	Good	Average	Poor
Kitchen	☐	☐	☐
Cabinets	☐	☐	☐
Countertop	☐	☐	☐
Counter Space	☐	☐	☐
Flooring	☐	☐	☐
Oven / Stove	☐	☐	☐
Microwave	☐	☐	☐
Layout	☐	☐	☐
Light Fixtures	☐	☐	☐
Backsplash	☐	☐	☐
Pantry	☐	☐	☐
Appliances	☐	☐	☐
Island	☐	☐	☐

	Good	Average	Poor
Basement	☐	☐	☐
Garage	☐	☐	☐

COMMUNITY

	Good	Average	Poor
Immediate Neighborhood	☐	☐	☐
Close to Employment	☐	☐	☐
Close to Shopping	☐	☐	☐
Close to Transportation	☐	☐	☐
Close to Schools / Daycare	☐	☐	☐
Close to Places of Worship	☐	☐	☐
Near Recreational Facilities	☐	☐	☐
Close to Airport	☐	☐	☐
Near Police and Fire Department	☐	☐	☐

Address ______________________ Price ______________

Bedrooms __________ Bathrooms __________ Sq.Ft. ______________

Lot Size: __________ Year Built __________ School District ________

Annual Tax __________

EXTERIOR

	Good	Average	Poor
View/Yard/Landscaping	☐	☐	☐
Trees	☐	☐	☐
Lawn (Front)	☐	☐	☐
Lawn (Back)	☐	☐	☐
Fences (condition)	☐	☐	☐
Landscaping (condition)	☐	☐	☐
Irrigation / Sprinkler	☐	☐	☐
	☐	☐	☐
House Type	☐	☐	☐
Exterior Siding	☐	☐	☐
Deck / Patio / Porch	☐	☐	☐
Garage	☐	☐	☐
Window / Doors	☐	☐	☐
Roof / Gutters	☐	☐	☐
Fencing	☐	☐	☐

HOME SYSTEMS

	Good	Average	Poor
Electrical	☐	☐	☐
Air Conditioning / Fans	☐	☐	☐
Heating	☐	☐	☐
Security	☐	☐	☐
Plumbing	☐	☐	☐
Intercom	☐	☐	☐

FEATURES

	Good	Average	Poor
Home Warranty	☐	☐	☐
Energy Saving Features	☐	☐	☐

INTERIOR

	Good	Average	Poor
Walls / Trim / Ceilings	☐	☐	☐
Flooring	☐	☐	☐
Stairs	☐	☐	☐
Storage	☐	☐	☐
Living Room	☐	☐	☐
Family Room	☐	☐	☐
Dining Room	☐	☐	☐

	Good	Average	Poor
Master Bedroom	☐	☐	☐
Bedroom 2	☐	☐	☐
Bedroom 3	☐	☐	☐
Bedroom 4	☐	☐	☐
Master Bathroom	☐	☐	☐
Bathroom 2	☐	☐	☐
Bathroom 3	☐	☐	☐
Bonus / Game Room	☐	☐	☐

	Good	Average	Poor
Kitchen	☐	☐	☐
Cabinets	☐	☐	☐
Countertop	☐	☐	☐
Counter Space	☐	☐	☐
Flooring	☐	☐	☐
Oven / Stove	☐	☐	☐
Microwave	☐	☐	☐
Layout	☐	☐	☐
Light Fixtures	☐	☐	☐
Backsplash	☐	☐	☐
Pantry	☐	☐	☐
Appliances	☐	☐	☐
Island	☐	☐	☐

	Good	Average	Poor
Basement	☐	☐	☐
Garage	☐	☐	☐

COMMUNITY

	Good	Average	Poor
Immediate Neighborhood	☐	☐	☐
Close to Employment	☐	☐	☐
Close to Shopping	☐	☐	☐
Close to Transportation	☐	☐	☐
Close to Schools / Daycare	☐	☐	☐
Close to Places of Worship	☐	☐	☐
Near Recreational Facilities	☐	☐	☐
Close to Airport	☐	☐	☐
Near Police and Fire Department	☐	☐	☐

Address ______________________________ Price ______________

Bedrooms __________ Bathrooms ___________ Sq.Ft. ______________

Lot Size: __________ Year Built ____________ School District _______

Annual Tax _________

EXTERIOR

	Good	Average	Poor
View/Yard/Landscaping	☐	☐	☐
Trees	☐	☐	☐
Lawn (Front)	☐	☐	☐
Lawn (Back)	☐	☐	☐
Fences (condition)	☐	☐	☐
Landscaping (condition)	☐	☐	☐
Irrigation / Sprinkler	☐	☐	☐
	☐	☐	☐
House Type	☐	☐	☐
Exterior Siding	☐	☐	☐
Deck / Patio / Porch	☐	☐	☐
Garage	☐	☐	☐
Window / Doors	☐	☐	☐
Roof / Gutters	☐	☐	☐
Fencing	☐	☐	☐

HOME SYSTEMS

	Good	Average	Poor
Electrical	☐	☐	☐
Air Conditioning / Fans	☐	☐	☐
Heating	☐	☐	☐
Security	☐	☐	☐
Plumbing	☐	☐	☐
Intercom	☐	☐	☐

FEATURES

	Good	Average	Poor
Home Warranty	☐	☐	☐
Energy Saving Features	☐	☐	☐

INTERIOR

	Good	Average	Poor
Walls / Trim / Ceilings	☐	☐	☐
Flooring	☐	☐	☐
Stairs	☐	☐	☐
Storage	☐	☐	☐
Living Room	☐	☐	☐
Family Room	☐	☐	☐
Dining Room	☐	☐	☐

	Good	Average	Poor
Master Bedroom	☐	☐	☐
Bedroom 2	☐	☐	☐
Bedroom 3	☐	☐	☐
Bedroom 4	☐	☐	☐
Master Bathroom	☐	☐	☐
Bathroom 2	☐	☐	☐
Bathroom 3	☐	☐	☐
Bonus / Game Room	☐	☐	☐

	Good	Average	Poor
Kitchen	☐	☐	☐
Cabinets	☐	☐	☐
Countertop	☐	☐	☐
Counter Space	☐	☐	☐
Flooring	☐	☐	☐
Oven / Stove	☐	☐	☐
Microwave	☐	☐	☐
Layout	☐	☐	☐
Light Fixtures	☐	☐	☐
Backsplash	☐	☐	☐
Pantry	☐	☐	☐
Appliances	☐	☐	☐
Island	☐	☐	☐

	Good	Average	Poor
Basement	☐	☐	☐
Garage	☐	☐	☐

COMMUNITY

	Good	Average	Poor
Immediate Neighborhood	☐	☐	☐
Close to Employment	☐	☐	☐
Close to Shopping	☐	☐	☐
Close to Transportation	☐	☐	☐
Close to Schools / Daycare	☐	☐	☐
Close to Places of Worship	☐	☐	☐
Near Recreational Facilities	☐	☐	☐
Close to Airport	☐	☐	☐
Near Police and Fire Department	☐	☐	☐

Address ____________________ Price ____________

Bedrooms ____________ Bathrooms ____________ Sq.Ft. ____________

Lot Size: ____________ Year Built ____________ School District ________

Annual Tax ____________

EXTERIOR

	Good	Average	Poor
View/Yard/Landscaping	☐	☐	☐
Trees	☐	☐	☐
Lawn (Front)	☐	☐	☐
Lawn (Back)	☐	☐	☐
Fences (condition)	☐	☐	☐
Landscaping (condition)	☐	☐	☐
Irrigation / Sprinkler	☐	☐	☐
	☐	☐	☐
House Type	☐	☐	☐
Exterior Siding	☐	☐	☐
Deck / Patio / Porch	☐	☐	☐
Garage	☐	☐	☐
Window / Doors	☐	☐	☐
Roof / Gutters	☐	☐	☐
Fencing	☐	☐	☐

HOME SYSTEMS

	Good	Average	Poor
Electrical	☐	☐	☐
Air Conditioning / Fans	☐	☐	☐
Heating	☐	☐	☐
Security	☐	☐	☐
Plumbing	☐	☐	☐
Intercom	☐	☐	☐

FEATURES

	Good	Average	Poor
Home Warranty	☐	☐	☐
Energy Saving Features	☐	☐	☐

INTERIOR

	Good	Average	Poor
Walls / Trim / Ceilings	☐	☐	☐
Flooring	☐	☐	☐
Stairs	☐	☐	☐
Storage	☐	☐	☐
Living Room	☐	☐	☐
Family Room	☐	☐	☐
Dining Room	☐	☐	☐

	Good	Average	Poor
Master Bedroom	☐	☐	☐
Bedroom 2	☐	☐	☐
Bedroom 3	☐	☐	☐
Bedroom 4	☐	☐	☐
Master Bathroom	☐	☐	☐
Bathroom 2	☐	☐	☐
Bathroom 3	☐	☐	☐
Bonus / Game Room	☐	☐	☐

	Good	Average	Poor
Kitchen	☐	☐	☐
Cabinets	☐	☐	☐
Countertop	☐	☐	☐
Counter Space	☐	☐	☐
Flooring	☐	☐	☐
Oven / Stove	☐	☐	☐
Microwave	☐	☐	☐
Layout	☐	☐	☐
Light Fixtures	☐	☐	☐
Backsplash	☐	☐	☐
Pantry	☐	☐	☐
Appliances	☐	☐	☐
Island	☐	☐	☐

	Good	Average	Poor
Basement	☐	☐	☐
Garage	☐	☐	☐

COMMUNITY

	Good	Average	Poor
Immediate Neighborhood	☐	☐	☐
Close to Employment	☐	☐	☐
Close to Shopping	☐	☐	☐
Close to Transportation	☐	☐	☐
Close to Schools / Daycare	☐	☐	☐
Close to Places of Worship	☐	☐	☐
Near Recreational Facilities	☐	☐	☐
Close to Airport	☐	☐	☐
Near Police and Fire Department	☐	☐	☐

Address ______________________ Price ______________

Bedrooms ____________ Bathrooms ____________ Sq.Ft. ______________

Lot Size: ____________ Year Built ____________ School District ________

Annual Tax ____________

EXTERIOR

	Good	Average	Poor
View/Yard/Landscaping	☐	☐	☐
Trees	☐	☐	☐
Lawn (Front)	☐	☐	☐
Lawn (Back)	☐	☐	☐
Fences (condition)	☐	☐	☐
Landscaping (condition)	☐	☐	☐
Irrigation / Sprinkler	☐	☐	☐
	☐	☐	☐
House Type	☐	☐	☐
Exterior Siding	☐	☐	☐
Deck / Patio / Porch	☐	☐	☐
Garage	☐	☐	☐
Window / Doors	☐	☐	☐
Roof / Gutters	☐	☐	☐
Fencing	☐	☐	☐

HOME SYSTEMS

	Good	Average	Poor
Electrical	☐	☐	☐
Air Conditioning / Fans	☐	☐	☐
Heating	☐	☐	☐
Security	☐	☐	☐
Plumbing	☐	☐	☐
Intercom	☐	☐	☐

FEATURES

	Good	Average	Poor
Home Warranty	☐	☐	☐
Energy Saving Features	☐	☐	☐

INTERIOR

	Good	Average	Poor
Walls / Trim / Ceilings	☐	☐	☐
Flooring	☐	☐	☐
Stairs	☐	☐	☐
Storage	☐	☐	☐
Living Room	☐	☐	☐
Family Room	☐	☐	☐
Dining Room	☐	☐	☐

	Good	Average	Poor
Master Bedroom	☐	☐	☐
Bedroom 2	☐	☐	☐
Bedroom 3	☐	☐	☐
Bedroom 4	☐	☐	☐
Master Bathroom	☐	☐	☐
Bathroom 2	☐	☐	☐
Bathroom 3	☐	☐	☐
Bonus / Game Room	☐	☐	☐

	Good	Average	Poor
Kitchen	☐	☐	☐
Cabinets	☐	☐	☐
Countertop	☐	☐	☐
Counter Space	☐	☐	☐
Flooring	☐	☐	☐
Oven / Stove	☐	☐	☐
Microwave	☐	☐	☐
Layout	☐	☐	☐
Light Fixtures	☐	☐	☐
Backsplash	☐	☐	☐
Pantry	☐	☐	☐
Appliances	☐	☐	☐
Island	☐	☐	☐

	Good	Average	Poor
Basement	☐	☐	☐
Garage	☐	☐	☐

COMMUNITY

	Good	Average	Poor
Immediate Neighborhood	☐	☐	☐
Close to Employment	☐	☐	☐
Close to Shopping	☐	☐	☐
Close to Transportation	☐	☐	☐
Close to Schools / Daycare	☐	☐	☐
Close to Places of Worship	☐	☐	☐
Near Recreational Facilities	☐	☐	☐
Close to Airport	☐	☐	☐
Near Police and Fire Department	☐	☐	☐

Address ______________________ Price ______________

Bedrooms ___________ Bathrooms ___________ Sq.Ft. ______________

Lot Size: ___________ Year Built ___________ School District _______

Annual Tax _________

EXTERIOR

	Good	Average	Poor
View/Yard/Landscaping	☐	☐	☐
Trees	☐	☐	☐
Lawn (Front)	☐	☐	☐
Lawn (Back)	☐	☐	☐
Fences (condition)	☐	☐	☐
Landscaping (condition)	☐	☐	☐
Irrigation / Sprinkler	☐	☐	☐
	☐	☐	☐
House Type	☐	☐	☐
Exterior Siding	☐	☐	☐
Deck / Patio / Porch	☐	☐	☐
Garage	☐	☐	☐
Window / Doors	☐	☐	☐
Roof / Gutters	☐	☐	☐
Fencing	☐	☐	☐

HOME SYSTEMS

	Good	Average	Poor
Electrical	☐	☐	☐
Air Conditioning / Fans	☐	☐	☐
Heating	☐	☐	☐
Security	☐	☐	☐
Plumbing	☐	☐	☐
Intercom	☐	☐	☐

FEATURES

	Good	Average	Poor
Home Warranty	☐	☐	☐
Energy Saving Features	☐	☐	☐

INTERIOR

	Good	Average	Poor
Walls / Trim / Ceilings	☐	☐	☐
Flooring	☐	☐	☐
Stairs	☐	☐	☐
Storage	☐	☐	☐
Living Room	☐	☐	☐
Family Room	☐	☐	☐
Dining Room	☐	☐	☐

	Good	Average	Poor
Master Bedroom	☐	☐	☐
Bedroom 2	☐	☐	☐
Bedroom 3	☐	☐	☐
Bedroom 4	☐	☐	☐
Master Bathroom	☐	☐	☐
Bathroom 2	☐	☐	☐
Bathroom 3	☐	☐	☐
Bonus / Game Room	☐	☐	☐

	Good	Average	Poor
Kitchen	☐	☐	☐
Cabinets	☐	☐	☐
Countertop	☐	☐	☐
Counter Space	☐	☐	☐
Flooring	☐	☐	☐
Oven / Stove	☐	☐	☐
Microwave	☐	☐	☐
Layout	☐	☐	☐
Light Fixtures	☐	☐	☐
Backsplash	☐	☐	☐
Pantry	☐	☐	☐
Appliances	☐	☐	☐
Island	☐	☐	☐

	Good	Average	Poor
Basement	☐	☐	☐
Garage	☐	☐	☐

COMMUNITY

	Good	Average	Poor
Immediate Neighborhood	☐	☐	☐
Close to Employment	☐	☐	☐
Close to Shopping	☐	☐	☐
Close to Transportation	☐	☐	☐
Close to Schools / Daycare	☐	☐	☐
Close to Places of Worship	☐	☐	☐
Near Recreational Facilities	☐	☐	☐
Close to Airport	☐	☐	☐
Near Police and Fire Department	☐	☐	☐

Address ______________________ Price ______________

Bedrooms __________ Bathrooms __________ Sq.Ft. ______________

Lot Size: __________ Year Built __________ School District ______

Annual Tax __________

EXTERIOR

	Good	Average	Poor
View/Yard/Landscaping	☐	☐	☐
Trees	☐	☐	☐
Lawn (Front)	☐	☐	☐
Lawn (Back)	☐	☐	☐
Fences (condition)	☐	☐	☐
Landscaping (condition)	☐	☐	☐
Irrigation / Sprinkler	☐	☐	☐
	☐	☐	☐
House Type	☐	☐	☐
Exterior Siding	☐	☐	☐
Deck / Patio / Porch	☐	☐	☐
Garage	☐	☐	☐
Window / Doors	☐	☐	☐
Roof / Gutters	☐	☐	☐
Fencing	☐	☐	☐

HOME SYSTEMS

	Good	Average	Poor
Electrical	☐	☐	☐
Air Conditioning / Fans	☐	☐	☐
Heating	☐	☐	☐
Security	☐	☐	☐
Plumbing	☐	☐	☐
Intercom	☐	☐	☐

FEATURES

	Good	Average	Poor
Home Warranty	☐	☐	☐
Energy Saving Features	☐	☐	☐

INTERIOR

	Good	Average	Poor
Walls / Trim / Ceilings	☐	☐	☐
Flooring	☐	☐	☐
Stairs	☐	☐	☐
Storage	☐	☐	☐
Living Room	☐	☐	☐
Family Room	☐	☐	☐
Dining Room	☐	☐	☐

	Good	Average	Poor
Master Bedroom	☐	☐	☐
Bedroom 2	☐	☐	☐
Bedroom 3	☐	☐	☐
Bedroom 4	☐	☐	☐
Master Bathroom	☐	☐	☐
Bathroom 2	☐	☐	☐
Bathroom 3	☐	☐	☐
Bonus / Game Room	☐	☐	☐

	Good	Average	Poor
Kitchen	☐	☐	☐
Cabinets	☐	☐	☐
Countertop	☐	☐	☐
Counter Space	☐	☐	☐
Flooring	☐	☐	☐
Oven / Stove	☐	☐	☐
Microwave	☐	☐	☐
Layout	☐	☐	☐
Light Fixtures	☐	☐	☐
Backsplash	☐	☐	☐
Pantry	☐	☐	☐
Appliances	☐	☐	☐
Island	☐	☐	☐

	Good	Average	Poor
Basement	☐	☐	☐
Garage	☐	☐	☐

COMMUNITY

	Good	Average	Poor
Immediate Neighborhood	☐	☐	☐
Close to Employment	☐	☐	☐
Close to Shopping	☐	☐	☐
Close to Transportation	☐	☐	☐
Close to Schools / Daycare	☐	☐	☐
Close to Places of Worship	☐	☐	☐
Near Recreational Facilities	☐	☐	☐
Close to Airport	☐	☐	☐
Near Police and Fire Department	☐	☐	☐

Address ______________________ Price ____________

Bedrooms ____________ Bathrooms ____________ Sq.Ft. ____________

Lot Size: ____________ Year Built ____________ School District ________

Annual Tax ________

EXTERIOR

	Good	Average	Poor
View/Yard/Landscaping	☐	☐	☐
Trees	☐	☐	☐
Lawn (Front)	☐	☐	☐
Lawn (Back)	☐	☐	☐
Fences (condition)	☐	☐	☐
Landscaping (condition)	☐	☐	☐
Irrigation / Sprinkler	☐	☐	☐
	☐	☐	☐
House Type	☐	☐	☐
Exterior Siding	☐	☐	☐
Deck / Patio / Porch	☐	☐	☐
Garage	☐	☐	☐
Window / Doors	☐	☐	☐
Roof / Gutters	☐	☐	☐
Fencing	☐	☐	☐

HOME SYSTEMS

	Good	Average	Poor
Electrical	☐	☐	☐
Air Conditioning / Fans	☐	☐	☐
Heating	☐	☐	☐
Security	☐	☐	☐
Plumbing	☐	☐	☐
Intercom	☐	☐	☐

FEATURES

	Good	Average	Poor
Home Warranty	☐	☐	☐
Energy Saving Features	☐	☐	☐

INTERIOR

	Good	Average	Poor
Walls / Trim / Ceilings	☐	☐	☐
Flooring	☐	☐	☐
Stairs	☐	☐	☐
Storage	☐	☐	☐
Living Room	☐	☐	☐
Family Room	☐	☐	☐
Dining Room	☐	☐	☐

	Good	Average	Poor
Master Bedroom	☐	☐	☐
Bedroom 2	☐	☐	☐
Bedroom 3	☐	☐	☐
Bedroom 4	☐	☐	☐
Master Bathroom	☐	☐	☐
Bathroom 2	☐	☐	☐
Bathroom 3	☐	☐	☐
Bonus / Game Room	☐	☐	☐

	Good	Average	Poor
Kitchen	☐	☐	☐
Cabinets	☐	☐	☐
Countertop	☐	☐	☐
Counter Space	☐	☐	☐
Flooring	☐	☐	☐
Oven / Stove	☐	☐	☐
Microwave	☐	☐	☐
Layout	☐	☐	☐
Light Fixtures	☐	☐	☐
Backsplash	☐	☐	☐
Pantry	☐	☐	☐
Appliances	☐	☐	☐
Island	☐	☐	☐

	Good	Average	Poor
Basement	☐	☐	☐
Garage	☐	☐	☐

COMMUNITY

	Good	Average	Poor
Immediate Neighborhood	☐	☐	☐
Close to Employment	☐	☐	☐
Close to Shopping	☐	☐	☐
Close to Transportation	☐	☐	☐
Close to Schools / Daycare	☐	☐	☐
Close to Places of Worship	☐	☐	☐
Near Recreational Facilities	☐	☐	☐
Close to Airport	☐	☐	☐
Near Police and Fire Department	☐	☐	☐

Address ______________________ Price ______________

Bedrooms ____________ Bathrooms ____________ Sq.Ft. ______________

Lot Size: ____________ Year Built ____________ School District ________

Annual Tax ____________

EXTERIOR

	Good	Average	Poor
View/Yard/Landscaping	☐	☐	☐
Trees	☐	☐	☐
Lawn (Front)	☐	☐	☐
Lawn (Back)	☐	☐	☐
Fences (condition)	☐	☐	☐
Landscaping (condition)	☐	☐	☐
Irrigation / Sprinkler	☐	☐	☐
	☐	☐	☐
House Type	☐	☐	☐
Exterior Siding	☐	☐	☐
Deck / Patio / Porch	☐	☐	☐
Garage	☐	☐	☐
Window / Doors	☐	☐	☐
Roof / Gutters	☐	☐	☐
Fencing	☐	☐	☐

HOME SYSTEMS

	Good	Average	Poor
Electrical	☐	☐	☐
Air Conditioning / Fans	☐	☐	☐
Heating	☐	☐	☐
Security	☐	☐	☐
Plumbing	☐	☐	☐
Intercom	☐	☐	☐

FEATURES

	Good	Average	Poor
Home Warranty	☐	☐	☐
Energy Saving Features	☐	☐	☐

INTERIOR

	Good	Average	Poor
Walls / Trim / Ceilings	☐	☐	☐
Flooring	☐	☐	☐
Stairs	☐	☐	☐
Storage	☐	☐	☐
Living Room	☐	☐	☐
Family Room	☐	☐	☐
Dining Room	☐	☐	☐

	Good	Average	Poor
Master Bedroom	☐	☐	☐
Bedroom 2	☐	☐	☐
Bedroom 3	☐	☐	☐
Bedroom 4	☐	☐	☐
Master Bathroom	☐	☐	☐
Bathroom 2	☐	☐	☐
Bathroom 3	☐	☐	☐
Bonus / Game Room	☐	☐	☐

	Good	Average	Poor
Kitchen	☐	☐	☐
Cabinets	☐	☐	☐
Countertop	☐	☐	☐
Counter Space	☐	☐	☐
Flooring	☐	☐	☐
Oven / Stove	☐	☐	☐
Microwave	☐	☐	☐
Layout	☐	☐	☐
Light Fixtures	☐	☐	☐
Backsplash	☐	☐	☐
Pantry	☐	☐	☐
Appliances	☐	☐	☐
Island	☐	☐	☐

	Good	Average	Poor
Basement	☐	☐	☐
Garage	☐	☐	☐

COMMUNITY

	Good	Average	Poor
Immediate Neighborhood	☐	☐	☐
Close to Employment	☐	☐	☐
Close to Shopping	☐	☐	☐
Close to Transportation	☐	☐	☐
Close to Schools / Daycare	☐	☐	☐
Close to Places of Worship	☐	☐	☐
Near Recreational Facilities	☐	☐	☐
Close to Airport	☐	☐	☐
Near Police and Fire Department	☐	☐	☐

Address ______________________ Price ______________

Bedrooms __________ Bathrooms __________ Sq.Ft. ______________

Lot Size: __________ Year Built __________ School District ________

Annual Tax __________

EXTERIOR

	Good	Average	Poor
View/Yard/Landscaping	☐	☐	☐
Trees	☐	☐	☐
Lawn (Front)	☐	☐	☐
Lawn (Back)	☐	☐	☐
Fences (condition)	☐	☐	☐
Landscaping (condition)	☐	☐	☐
Irrigation / Sprinkler	☐	☐	☐
	☐	☐	☐
House Type	☐	☐	☐
Exterior Siding	☐	☐	☐
Deck / Patio / Porch	☐	☐	☐
Garage	☐	☐	☐
Window / Doors	☐	☐	☐
Roof / Gutters	☐	☐	☐
Fencing	☐	☐	☐

HOME SYSTEMS

	Good	Average	Poor
Electrical	☐	☐	☐
Air Conditioning / Fans	☐	☐	☐
Heating	☐	☐	☐
Security	☐	☐	☐
Plumbing	☐	☐	☐
Intercom	☐	☐	☐

FEATURES

	Good	Average	Poor
Home Warranty	☐	☐	☐
Energy Saving Features	☐	☐	☐

INTERIOR

	Good	Average	Poor
Walls / Trim / Ceilings	☐	☐	☐
Flooring	☐	☐	☐
Stairs	☐	☐	☐
Storage	☐	☐	☐
Living Room	☐	☐	☐
Family Room	☐	☐	☐
Dining Room	☐	☐	☐

	Good	Average	Poor
Master Bedroom	☐	☐	☐
Bedroom 2	☐	☐	☐
Bedroom 3	☐	☐	☐
Bedroom 4	☐	☐	☐
Master Bathroom	☐	☐	☐
Bathroom 2	☐	☐	☐
Bathroom 3	☐	☐	☐
Bonus / Game Room	☐	☐	☐

	Good	Average	Poor
Kitchen	☐	☐	☐
Cabinets	☐	☐	☐
Countertop	☐	☐	☐
Counter Space	☐	☐	☐
Flooring	☐	☐	☐
Oven / Stove	☐	☐	☐
Microwave	☐	☐	☐
Layout	☐	☐	☐
Light Fixtures	☐	☐	☐
Backsplash	☐	☐	☐
Pantry	☐	☐	☐
Appliances	☐	☐	☐
Island	☐	☐	☐

	Good	Average	Poor
Basement	☐	☐	☐
Garage	☐	☐	☐

COMMUNITY

	Good	Average	Poor
Immediate Neighborhood	☐	☐	☐
Close to Employment	☐	☐	☐
Close to Shopping	☐	☐	☐
Close to Transportation	☐	☐	☐
Close to Schools / Daycare	☐	☐	☐
Close to Places of Worship	☐	☐	☐
Near Recreational Facilities	☐	☐	☐
Close to Airport	☐	☐	☐
Near Police and Fire Department	☐	☐	☐

Address ______________________ Price ______________

Bedrooms ________ Bathrooms ________ Sq.Ft. ______________

Lot Size: ________ Year Built ________ School District ________

Annual Tax ________

EXTERIOR

	Good	Average	Poor
View/Yard/Landscaping	☐	☐	☐
Trees	☐	☐	☐
Lawn (Front)	☐	☐	☐
Lawn (Back)	☐	☐	☐
Fences (condition)	☐	☐	☐
Landscaping (condition)	☐	☐	☐
Irrigation / Sprinkler	☐	☐	☐
	☐	☐	☐
House Type	☐	☐	☐
Exterior Siding	☐	☐	☐
Deck / Patio / Porch	☐	☐	☐
Garage	☐	☐	☐
Window / Doors	☐	☐	☐
Roof / Gutters	☐	☐	☐
Fencing	☐	☐	☐

HOME SYSTEMS

	Good	Average	Poor
Electrical	☐	☐	☐
Air Conditioning / Fans	☐	☐	☐
Heating	☐	☐	☐
Security	☐	☐	☐
Plumbing	☐	☐	☐
Intercom	☐	☐	☐

FEATURES

	Good	Average	Poor
Home Warranty	☐	☐	☐
Energy Saving Features	☐	☐	☐

INTERIOR

	Good	Average	Poor
Walls / Trim / Ceilings	☐	☐	☐
Flooring	☐	☐	☐
Stairs	☐	☐	☐
Storage	☐	☐	☐
Living Room	☐	☐	☐
Family Room	☐	☐	☐
Dining Room	☐	☐	☐

	Good	Average	Poor
Master Bedroom	☐	☐	☐
Bedroom 2	☐	☐	☐
Bedroom 3	☐	☐	☐
Bedroom 4	☐	☐	☐
Master Bathroom	☐	☐	☐
Bathroom 2	☐	☐	☐
Bathroom 3	☐	☐	☐
Bonus / Game Room	☐	☐	☐

	Good	Average	Poor
Kitchen	☐	☐	☐
Cabinets	☐	☐	☐
Countertop	☐	☐	☐
Counter Space	☐	☐	☐
Flooring	☐	☐	☐
Oven / Stove	☐	☐	☐
Microwave	☐	☐	☐
Layout	☐	☐	☐
Light Fixtures	☐	☐	☐
Backsplash	☐	☐	☐
Pantry	☐	☐	☐
Appliances	☐	☐	☐
Island	☐	☐	☐

	Good	Average	Poor
Basement	☐	☐	☐
Garage	☐	☐	☐

COMMUNITY

	Good	Average	Poor
Immediate Neighborhood	☐	☐	☐
Close to Employment	☐	☐	☐
Close to Shopping	☐	☐	☐
Close to Transportation	☐	☐	☐
Close to Schools / Daycare	☐	☐	☐
Close to Places of Worship	☐	☐	☐
Near Recreational Facilities	☐	☐	☐
Close to Airport	☐	☐	☐
Near Police and Fire Department	☐	☐	☐

Address ______________________________ Price ______________

Bedrooms __________ Bathrooms __________ Sq.Ft. ______________

Lot Size: __________ Year Built __________ School District _______

Annual Tax __________

EXTERIOR

	Good	Average	Poor
View/Yard/Landscaping	☐	☐	☐
Trees	☐	☐	☐
Lawn (Front)	☐	☐	☐
Lawn (Back)	☐	☐	☐
Fences (condition)	☐	☐	☐
Landscaping (condition)	☐	☐	☐
Irrigation / Sprinkler	☐	☐	☐
	☐	☐	☐
House Type	☐	☐	☐
Exterior Siding	☐	☐	☐
Deck / Patio / Porch	☐	☐	☐
Garage	☐	☐	☐
Window / Doors	☐	☐	☐
Roof / Gutters	☐	☐	☐
Fencing	☐	☐	☐

HOME SYSTEMS

	Good	Average	Poor
Electrical	☐	☐	☐
Air Conditioning / Fans	☐	☐	☐
Heating	☐	☐	☐
Security	☐	☐	☐
Plumbing	☐	☐	☐
Intercom	☐	☐	☐

FEATURES

	Good	Average	Poor
Home Warranty	☐	☐	☐
Energy Saving Features	☐	☐	☐

INTERIOR

	Good	Average	Poor
Walls / Trim / Ceilings	☐	☐	☐
Flooring	☐	☐	☐
Stairs	☐	☐	☐
Storage	☐	☐	☐
Living Room	☐	☐	☐
Family Room	☐	☐	☐
Dining Room	☐	☐	☐

	Good	Average	Poor
Master Bedroom	☐	☐	☐
Bedroom 2	☐	☐	☐
Bedroom 3	☐	☐	☐
Bedroom 4	☐	☐	☐
Master Bathroom	☐	☐	☐
Bathroom 2	☐	☐	☐
Bathroom 3	☐	☐	☐
Bonus / Game Room	☐	☐	☐

	Good	Average	Poor
Kitchen	☐	☐	☐
Cabinets	☐	☐	☐
Countertop	☐	☐	☐
Counter Space	☐	☐	☐
Flooring	☐	☐	☐
Oven / Stove	☐	☐	☐
Microwave	☐	☐	☐
Layout	☐	☐	☐
Light Fixtures	☐	☐	☐
Backsplash	☐	☐	☐
Pantry	☐	☐	☐
Appliances	☐	☐	☐
Island	☐	☐	☐

	Good	Average	Poor
Basement	☐	☐	☐
Garage	☐	☐	☐

COMMUNITY

	Good	Average	Poor
Immediate Neighborhood	☐	☐	☐
Close to Employment	☐	☐	☐
Close to Shopping	☐	☐	☐
Close to Transportation	☐	☐	☐
Close to Schools / Daycare	☐	☐	☐
Close to Places of Worship	☐	☐	☐
Near Recreational Facilities	☐	☐	☐
Close to Airport	☐	☐	☐
Near Police and Fire Department	☐	☐	☐

Address ______________________ Price ____________

Bedrooms ________ Bathrooms ________ Sq.Ft. ____________

Lot Size: ________ Year Built ________ School District ________

Annual Tax ________

EXTERIOR

	Good	Average	Poor
View/Yard/Landscaping	☐	☐	☐
Trees	☐	☐	☐
Lawn (Front)	☐	☐	☐
Lawn (Back)	☐	☐	☐
Fences (condition)	☐	☐	☐
Landscaping (condition)	☐	☐	☐
Irrigation / Sprinkler	☐	☐	☐
	☐	☐	☐
House Type	☐	☐	☐
Exterior Siding	☐	☐	☐
Deck / Patio / Porch	☐	☐	☐
Garage	☐	☐	☐
Window / Doors	☐	☐	☐
Roof / Gutters	☐	☐	☐
Fencing	☐	☐	☐

HOME SYSTEMS

	Good	Average	Poor
Electrical	☐	☐	☐
Air Conditioning / Fans	☐	☐	☐
Heating	☐	☐	☐
Security	☐	☐	☐
Plumbing	☐	☐	☐
Intercom	☐	☐	☐

FEATURES

	Good	Average	Poor
Home Warranty	☐	☐	☐
Energy Saving Features	☐	☐	☐

INTERIOR

	Good	Average	Poor
Walls / Trim / Ceilings	☐	☐	☐
Flooring	☐	☐	☐
Stairs	☐	☐	☐
Storage	☐	☐	☐
Living Room	☐	☐	☐
Family Room	☐	☐	☐
Dining Room	☐	☐	☐

	Good	Average	Poor
Master Bedroom	☐	☐	☐
Bedroom 2	☐	☐	☐
Bedroom 3	☐	☐	☐
Bedroom 4	☐	☐	☐
Master Bathroom	☐	☐	☐
Bathroom 2	☐	☐	☐
Bathroom 3	☐	☐	☐
Bonus / Game Room	☐	☐	☐

	Good	Average	Poor
Kitchen	☐	☐	☐
Cabinets	☐	☐	☐
Countertop	☐	☐	☐
Counter Space	☐	☐	☐
Flooring	☐	☐	☐
Oven / Stove	☐	☐	☐
Microwave	☐	☐	☐
Layout	☐	☐	☐
Light Fixtures	☐	☐	☐
Backsplash	☐	☐	☐
Pantry	☐	☐	☐
Appliances	☐	☐	☐
Island	☐	☐	☐

	Good	Average	Poor
Basement	☐	☐	☐
Garage	☐	☐	☐

COMMUNITY

	Good	Average	Poor
Immediate Neighborhood	☐	☐	☐
Close to Employment	☐	☐	☐
Close to Shopping	☐	☐	☐
Close to Transportation	☐	☐	☐
Close to Schools / Daycare	☐	☐	☐
Close to Places of Worship	☐	☐	☐
Near Recreational Facilities	☐	☐	☐
Close to Airport	☐	☐	☐
Near Police and Fire Department	☐	☐	☐

Address ______________________ Price ____________

Bedrooms ________ Bathrooms ________ Sq.Ft. ____________

Lot Size: ________ Year Built ________ School District ______

Annual Tax ________

EXTERIOR

	Good	Average	Poor
View/Yard/Landscaping	☐	☐	☐
Trees	☐	☐	☐
Lawn (Front)	☐	☐	☐
Lawn (Back)	☐	☐	☐
Fences (condition)	☐	☐	☐
Landscaping (condition)	☐	☐	☐
Irrigation / Sprinkler	☐	☐	☐
	☐	☐	☐
House Type	☐	☐	☐
Exterior Siding	☐	☐	☐
Deck / Patio / Porch	☐	☐	☐
Garage	☐	☐	☐
Window / Doors	☐	☐	☐
Roof / Gutters	☐	☐	☐
Fencing	☐	☐	☐

HOME SYSTEMS

	Good	Average	Poor
Electrical	☐	☐	☐
Air Conditioning / Fans	☐	☐	☐
Heating	☐	☐	☐
Security	☐	☐	☐
Plumbing	☐	☐	☐
Intercom	☐	☐	☐

FEATURES

	Good	Average	Poor
Home Warranty	☐	☐	☐
Energy Saving Features	☐	☐	☐

INTERIOR

	Good	Average	Poor
Walls / Trim / Ceilings	☐	☐	☐
Flooring	☐	☐	☐
Stairs	☐	☐	☐
Storage	☐	☐	☐
Living Room	☐	☐	☐
Family Room	☐	☐	☐
Dining Room	☐	☐	☐

	Good	Average	Poor
Master Bedroom	☐	☐	☐
Bedroom 2	☐	☐	☐
Bedroom 3	☐	☐	☐
Bedroom 4	☐	☐	☐
Master Bathroom	☐	☐	☐
Bathroom 2	☐	☐	☐
Bathroom 3	☐	☐	☐
Bonus / Game Room	☐	☐	☐

	Good	Average	Poor
Kitchen	☐	☐	☐
Cabinets	☐	☐	☐
Countertop	☐	☐	☐
Counter Space	☐	☐	☐
Flooring	☐	☐	☐
Oven / Stove	☐	☐	☐
Microwave	☐	☐	☐
Layout	☐	☐	☐
Light Fixtures	☐	☐	☐
Backsplash	☐	☐	☐
Pantry	☐	☐	☐
Appliances	☐	☐	☐
Island	☐	☐	☐

	Good	Average	Poor
Basement	☐	☐	☐
Garage	☐	☐	☐

COMMUNITY

	Good	Average	Poor
Immediate Neighborhood	☐	☐	☐
Close to Employment	☐	☐	☐
Close to Shopping	☐	☐	☐
Close to Transportation	☐	☐	☐
Close to Schools / Daycare	☐	☐	☐
Close to Places of Worship	☐	☐	☐
Near Recreational Facilities	☐	☐	☐
Close to Airport	☐	☐	☐
Near Police and Fire Department	☐	☐	☐

Address ______________________ Price ______________

Bedrooms __________ Bathrooms __________ Sq.Ft. ______________

Lot Size: __________ Year Built __________ School District ______

Annual Tax __________

EXTERIOR

	Good	Average	Poor
View/Yard/Landscaping	☐	☐	☐
Trees	☐	☐	☐
Lawn (Front)	☐	☐	☐
Lawn (Back)	☐	☐	☐
Fences (condition)	☐	☐	☐
Landscaping (condition)	☐	☐	☐
Irrigation / Sprinkler	☐	☐	☐
	☐	☐	☐
House Type	☐	☐	☐
Exterior Siding	☐	☐	☐
Deck / Patio / Porch	☐	☐	☐
Garage	☐	☐	☐
Window / Doors	☐	☐	☐
Roof / Gutters	☐	☐	☐
Fencing	☐	☐	☐

HOME SYSTEMS

	Good	Average	Poor
Electrical	☐	☐	☐
Air Conditioning / Fans	☐	☐	☐
Heating	☐	☐	☐
Security	☐	☐	☐
Plumbing	☐	☐	☐
Intercom	☐	☐	☐

FEATURES

	Good	Average	Poor
Home Warranty	☐	☐	☐
Energy Saving Features	☐	☐	☐

INTERIOR

	Good	Average	Poor
Walls / Trim / Ceilings	☐	☐	☐
Flooring	☐	☐	☐
Stairs	☐	☐	☐
Storage	☐	☐	☐
Living Room	☐	☐	☐
Family Room	☐	☐	☐
Dining Room	☐	☐	☐

	Good	Average	Poor
Master Bedroom	☐	☐	☐
Bedroom 2	☐	☐	☐
Bedroom 3	☐	☐	☐
Bedroom 4	☐	☐	☐
Master Bathroom	☐	☐	☐
Bathroom 2	☐	☐	☐
Bathroom 3	☐	☐	☐
Bonus / Game Room	☐	☐	☐

	Good	Average	Poor
Kitchen	☐	☐	☐
Cabinets	☐	☐	☐
Countertop	☐	☐	☐
Counter Space	☐	☐	☐
Flooring	☐	☐	☐
Oven / Stove	☐	☐	☐
Microwave	☐	☐	☐
Layout	☐	☐	☐
Light Fixtures	☐	☐	☐
Backsplash	☐	☐	☐
Pantry	☐	☐	☐
Appliances	☐	☐	☐
Island	☐	☐	☐

	Good	Average	Poor
Basement	☐	☐	☐
Garage	☐	☐	☐

COMMUNITY

	Good	Average	Poor
Immediate Neighborhood	☐	☐	☐
Close to Employment	☐	☐	☐
Close to Shopping	☐	☐	☐
Close to Transportation	☐	☐	☐
Close to Schools / Daycare	☐	☐	☐
Close to Places of Worship	☐	☐	☐
Near Recreational Facilities	☐	☐	☐
Close to Airport	☐	☐	☐
Near Police and Fire Department	☐	☐	☐

Address ______________________ Price ______________

Bedrooms ____________ Bathrooms ____________ Sq.Ft. ______________

Lot Size: ____________ Year Built ____________ School District ________

Annual Tax ____________

EXTERIOR

	Good	Average	Poor
View/Yard/Landscaping	☐	☐	☐
Trees	☐	☐	☐
Lawn (Front)	☐	☐	☐
Lawn (Back)	☐	☐	☐
Fences (condition)	☐	☐	☐
Landscaping (condition)	☐	☐	☐
Irrigation / Sprinkler	☐	☐	☐
	☐	☐	☐
House Type	☐	☐	☐
Exterior Siding	☐	☐	☐
Deck / Patio / Porch	☐	☐	☐
Garage	☐	☐	☐
Window / Doors	☐	☐	☐
Roof / Gutters	☐	☐	☐
Fencing	☐	☐	☐

HOME SYSTEMS

	Good	Average	Poor
Electrical	☐	☐	☐
Air Conditioning / Fans	☐	☐	☐
Heating	☐	☐	☐
Security	☐	☐	☐
Plumbing	☐	☐	☐
Intercom	☐	☐	☐

FEATURES

	Good	Average	Poor
Home Warranty	☐	☐	☐
Energy Saving Features	☐	☐	☐

INTERIOR

	Good	Average	Poor
Walls / Trim / Ceilings	☐	☐	☐
Flooring	☐	☐	☐
Stairs	☐	☐	☐
Storage	☐	☐	☐
Living Room	☐	☐	☐
Family Room	☐	☐	☐
Dining Room	☐	☐	☐

	Good	Average	Poor
Master Bedroom	☐	☐	☐
Bedroom 2	☐	☐	☐
Bedroom 3	☐	☐	☐
Bedroom 4	☐	☐	☐
Master Bathroom	☐	☐	☐
Bathroom 2	☐	☐	☐
Bathroom 3	☐	☐	☐
Bonus / Game Room	☐	☐	☐

	Good	Average	Poor
Kitchen	☐	☐	☐
Cabinets	☐	☐	☐
Countertop	☐	☐	☐
Counter Space	☐	☐	☐
Flooring	☐	☐	☐
Oven / Stove	☐	☐	☐
Microwave	☐	☐	☐
Layout	☐	☐	☐
Light Fixtures	☐	☐	☐
Backsplash	☐	☐	☐
Pantry	☐	☐	☐
Appliances	☐	☐	☐
Island	☐	☐	☐

	Good	Average	Poor
Basement	☐	☐	☐
Garage	☐	☐	☐

COMMUNITY

	Good	Average	Poor
Immediate Neighborhood	☐	☐	☐
Close to Employment	☐	☐	☐
Close to Shopping	☐	☐	☐
Close to Transportation	☐	☐	☐
Close to Schools / Daycare	☐	☐	☐
Close to Places of Worship	☐	☐	☐
Near Recreational Facilities	☐	☐	☐
Close to Airport	☐	☐	☐
Near Police and Fire Department	☐	☐	☐

Address ______________________ Price ______________

Bedrooms ____________ Bathrooms ____________ Sq.Ft. ______________

Lot Size: ____________ Year Built ____________ School District __________

Annual Tax ____________

EXTERIOR

	Good	Average	Poor
View/Yard/Landscaping	☐	☐	☐
Trees	☐	☐	☐
Lawn (Front)	☐	☐	☐
Lawn (Back)	☐	☐	☐
Fences (condition)	☐	☐	☐
Landscaping (condition)	☐	☐	☐
Irrigation / Sprinkler	☐	☐	☐
	☐	☐	☐
House Type	☐	☐	☐
Exterior Siding	☐	☐	☐
Deck / Patio / Porch	☐	☐	☐
Garage	☐	☐	☐
Window / Doors	☐	☐	☐
Roof / Gutters	☐	☐	☐
Fencing	☐	☐	☐

HOME SYSTEMS

	Good	Average	Poor
Electrical	☐	☐	☐
Air Conditioning / Fans	☐	☐	☐
Heating	☐	☐	☐
Security	☐	☐	☐
Plumbing	☐	☐	☐
Intercom	☐	☐	☐

FEATURES

	Good	Average	Poor
Home Warranty	☐	☐	☐
Energy Saving Features	☐	☐	☐

INTERIOR

	Good	Average	Poor
Walls / Trim / Ceilings	☐	☐	☐
Flooring	☐	☐	☐
Stairs	☐	☐	☐
Storage	☐	☐	☐
Living Room	☐	☐	☐
Family Room	☐	☐	☐
Dining Room	☐	☐	☐

	Good	Average	Poor
Master Bedroom	☐	☐	☐
Bedroom 2	☐	☐	☐
Bedroom 3	☐	☐	☐
Bedroom 4	☐	☐	☐
Master Bathroom	☐	☐	☐
Bathroom 2	☐	☐	☐
Bathroom 3	☐	☐	☐
Bonus / Game Room	☐	☐	☐

	Good	Average	Poor
Kitchen	☐	☐	☐
Cabinets	☐	☐	☐
Countertop	☐	☐	☐
Counter Space	☐	☐	☐
Flooring	☐	☐	☐
Oven / Stove	☐	☐	☐
Microwave	☐	☐	☐
Layout	☐	☐	☐
Light Fixtures	☐	☐	☐
Backsplash	☐	☐	☐
Pantry	☐	☐	☐
Appliances	☐	☐	☐
Island	☐	☐	☐

	Good	Average	Poor
Basement	☐	☐	☐
Garage	☐	☐	☐

COMMUNITY

	Good	Average	Poor
Immediate Neighborhood	☐	☐	☐
Close to Employment	☐	☐	☐
Close to Shopping	☐	☐	☐
Close to Transportation	☐	☐	☐
Close to Schools / Daycare	☐	☐	☐
Close to Places of Worship	☐	☐	☐
Near Recreational Facilities	☐	☐	☐
Close to Airport	☐	☐	☐
Near Police and Fire Department	☐	☐	☐

Address ______________________ Price ______________

Bedrooms __________ Bathrooms __________ Sq.Ft. ______________

Lot Size: __________ Year Built __________ School District __________

Annual Tax __________

EXTERIOR

	Good	Average	Poor
View/Yard/Landscaping	☐	☐	☐
Trees	☐	☐	☐
Lawn (Front)	☐	☐	☐
Lawn (Back)	☐	☐	☐
Fences (condition)	☐	☐	☐
Landscaping (condition)	☐	☐	☐
Irrigation / Sprinkler	☐	☐	☐
	☐	☐	☐
House Type	☐	☐	☐
Exterior Siding	☐	☐	☐
Deck / Patio / Porch	☐	☐	☐
Garage	☐	☐	☐
Window / Doors	☐	☐	☐
Roof / Gutters	☐	☐	☐
Fencing	☐	☐	☐

HOME SYSTEMS

	Good	Average	Poor
Electrical	☐	☐	☐
Air Conditioning / Fans	☐	☐	☐
Heating	☐	☐	☐
Security	☐	☐	☐
Plumbing	☐	☐	☐
Intercom	☐	☐	☐

FEATURES

	Good	Average	Poor
Home Warranty	☐	☐	☐
Energy Saving Features	☐	☐	☐

INTERIOR

	Good	Average	Poor
Walls / Trim / Ceilings	☐	☐	☐
Flooring	☐	☐	☐
Stairs	☐	☐	☐
Storage	☐	☐	☐
Living Room	☐	☐	☐
Family Room	☐	☐	☐
Dining Room	☐	☐	☐

	Good	Average	Poor
Master Bedroom	☐	☐	☐
Bedroom 2	☐	☐	☐
Bedroom 3	☐	☐	☐
Bedroom 4	☐	☐	☐
Master Bathroom	☐	☐	☐
Bathroom 2	☐	☐	☐
Bathroom 3	☐	☐	☐
Bonus / Game Room	☐	☐	☐

	Good	Average	Poor
Kitchen	☐	☐	☐
Cabinets	☐	☐	☐
Countertop	☐	☐	☐
Counter Space	☐	☐	☐
Flooring	☐	☐	☐
Oven / Stove	☐	☐	☐
Microwave	☐	☐	☐
Layout	☐	☐	☐
Light Fixtures	☐	☐	☐
Backsplash	☐	☐	☐
Pantry	☐	☐	☐
Appliances	☐	☐	☐
Island	☐	☐	☐

	Good	Average	Poor
Basement	☐	☐	☐
Garage	☐	☐	☐

COMMUNITY

	Good	Average	Poor
Immediate Neighborhood	☐	☐	☐
Close to Employment	☐	☐	☐
Close to Shopping	☐	☐	☐
Close to Transportation	☐	☐	☐
Close to Schools / Daycare	☐	☐	☐
Close to Places of Worship	☐	☐	☐
Near Recreational Facilities	☐	☐	☐
Close to Airport	☐	☐	☐
Near Police and Fire Department	☐	☐	☐

Address ______________________ Price ____________

Bedrooms ____________ Bathrooms ____________ Sq.Ft. ____________

Lot Size: ____________ Year Built ____________ School District ____________

Annual Tax ____________

EXTERIOR

	Good	Average	Poor
View/Yard/Landscaping	☐	☐	☐
Trees	☐	☐	☐
Lawn (Front)	☐	☐	☐
Lawn (Back)	☐	☐	☐
Fences (condition)	☐	☐	☐
Landscaping (condition)	☐	☐	☐
Irrigation / Sprinkler	☐	☐	☐
	☐	☐	☐
House Type	☐	☐	☐
Exterior Siding	☐	☐	☐
Deck / Patio / Porch	☐	☐	☐
Garage	☐	☐	☐
Window / Doors	☐	☐	☐
Roof / Gutters	☐	☐	☐
Fencing	☐	☐	☐

HOME SYSTEMS

	Good	Average	Poor
Electrical	☐	☐	☐
Air Conditioning / Fans	☐	☐	☐
Heating	☐	☐	☐
Security	☐	☐	☐
Plumbing	☐	☐	☐
Intercom	☐	☐	☐

FEATURES

	Good	Average	Poor
Home Warranty	☐	☐	☐
Energy Saving Features	☐	☐	☐

INTERIOR

	Good	Average	Poor
Walls / Trim / Ceilings	☐	☐	☐
Flooring	☐	☐	☐
Stairs	☐	☐	☐
Storage	☐	☐	☐
Living Room	☐	☐	☐
Family Room	☐	☐	☐
Dining Room	☐	☐	☐

	Good	Average	Poor
Master Bedroom	☐	☐	☐
Bedroom 2	☐	☐	☐
Bedroom 3	☐	☐	☐
Bedroom 4	☐	☐	☐
Master Bathroom	☐	☐	☐
Bathroom 2	☐	☐	☐
Bathroom 3	☐	☐	☐
Bonus / Game Room	☐	☐	☐

	Good	Average	Poor
Kitchen	☐	☐	☐
Cabinets	☐	☐	☐
Countertop	☐	☐	☐
Counter Space	☐	☐	☐
Flooring	☐	☐	☐
Oven / Stove	☐	☐	☐
Microwave	☐	☐	☐
Layout	☐	☐	☐
Light Fixtures	☐	☐	☐
Backsplash	☐	☐	☐
Pantry	☐	☐	☐
Appliances	☐	☐	☐
Island	☐	☐	☐

	Good	Average	Poor
Basement	☐	☐	☐
Garage	☐	☐	☐

COMMUNITY

	Good	Average	Poor
Immediate Neighborhood	☐	☐	☐
Close to Employment	☐	☐	☐
Close to Shopping	☐	☐	☐
Close to Transportation	☐	☐	☐
Close to Schools / Daycare	☐	☐	☐
Close to Places of Worship	☐	☐	☐
Near Recreational Facilities	☐	☐	☐
Close to Airport	☐	☐	☐
Near Police and Fire Department	☐	☐	☐

Address ______________ Price ______________

Bedrooms ______________ Bathrooms ______________ Sq.Ft. ______________

Lot Size: ______________ Year Built ______________ School District ______________

Annual Tax ______________

EXTERIOR

	Good	Average	Poor
View/Yard/Landscaping	☐	☐	☐
Trees	☐	☐	☐
Lawn (Front)	☐	☐	☐
Lawn (Back)	☐	☐	☐
Fences (condition)	☐	☐	☐
Landscaping (condition)	☐	☐	☐
Irrigation / Sprinkler	☐	☐	☐
	☐	☐	☐
House Type	☐	☐	☐
Exterior Siding	☐	☐	☐
Deck / Patio / Porch	☐	☐	☐
Garage	☐	☐	☐
Window / Doors	☐	☐	☐
Roof / Gutters	☐	☐	☐
Fencing	☐	☐	☐

HOME SYSTEMS

	Good	Average	Poor
Electrical	☐	☐	☐
Air Conditioning / Fans	☐	☐	☐
Heating	☐	☐	☐
Security	☐	☐	☐
Plumbing	☐	☐	☐
Intercom	☐	☐	☐

FEATURES

	Good	Average	Poor
Home Warranty	☐	☐	☐
Energy Saving Features	☐	☐	☐

INTERIOR

	Good	Average	Poor
Walls / Trim / Ceilings	☐	☐	☐
Flooring	☐	☐	☐
Stairs	☐	☐	☐
Storage	☐	☐	☐
Living Room	☐	☐	☐
Family Room	☐	☐	☐
Dining Room	☐	☐	☐

	Good	Average	Poor
Master Bedroom	☐	☐	☐
Bedroom 2	☐	☐	☐
Bedroom 3	☐	☐	☐
Bedroom 4	☐	☐	☐
Master Bathroom	☐	☐	☐
Bathroom 2	☐	☐	☐
Bathroom 3	☐	☐	☐
Bonus / Game Room	☐	☐	☐

	Good	Average	Poor
Kitchen	☐	☐	☐
Cabinets	☐	☐	☐
Countertop	☐	☐	☐
Counter Space	☐	☐	☐
Flooring	☐	☐	☐
Oven / Stove	☐	☐	☐
Microwave	☐	☐	☐
Layout	☐	☐	☐
Light Fixtures	☐	☐	☐
Backsplash	☐	☐	☐
Pantry	☐	☐	☐
Appliances	☐	☐	☐
Island	☐	☐	☐

	Good	Average	Poor
Basement	☐	☐	☐
Garage	☐	☐	☐

COMMUNITY

	Good	Average	Poor
Immediate Neighborhood	☐	☐	☐
Close to Employment	☐	☐	☐
Close to Shopping	☐	☐	☐
Close to Transportation	☐	☐	☐
Close to Schools / Daycare	☐	☐	☐
Close to Places of Worship	☐	☐	☐
Near Recreational Facilities	☐	☐	☐
Close to Airport	☐	☐	☐
Near Police and Fire Department	☐	☐	☐

Address ______________________ Price ____________

Bedrooms ________ Bathrooms ________ Sq.Ft. ____________

Lot Size: ________ Year Built ________ School District ______

Annual Tax ________

EXTERIOR

	Good	Average	Poor
View/Yard/Landscaping	☐	☐	☐
Trees	☐	☐	☐
Lawn (Front)	☐	☐	☐
Lawn (Back)	☐	☐	☐
Fences (condition)	☐	☐	☐
Landscaping (condition)	☐	☐	☐
Irrigation / Sprinkler	☐	☐	☐
	☐	☐	☐
House Type	☐	☐	☐
Exterior Siding	☐	☐	☐
Deck / Patio / Porch	☐	☐	☐
Garage	☐	☐	☐
Window / Doors	☐	☐	☐
Roof / Gutters	☐	☐	☐
Fencing	☐	☐	☐

HOME SYSTEMS

	Good	Average	Poor
Electrical	☐	☐	☐
Air Conditioning / Fans	☐	☐	☐
Heating	☐	☐	☐
Security	☐	☐	☐
Plumbing	☐	☐	☐
Intercom	☐	☐	☐

FEATURES

	Good	Average	Poor
Home Warranty	☐	☐	☐
Energy Saving Features	☐	☐	☐

INTERIOR

	Good	Average	Poor
Walls / Trim / Ceilings	☐	☐	☐
Flooring	☐	☐	☐
Stairs	☐	☐	☐
Storage	☐	☐	☐
Living Room	☐	☐	☐
Family Room	☐	☐	☐
Dining Room	☐	☐	☐

	Good	Average	Poor
Master Bedroom	☐	☐	☐
Bedroom 2	☐	☐	☐
Bedroom 3	☐	☐	☐
Bedroom 4	☐	☐	☐
Master Bathroom	☐	☐	☐
Bathroom 2	☐	☐	☐
Bathroom 3	☐	☐	☐
Bonus / Game Room	☐	☐	☐

	Good	Average	Poor
Kitchen	☐	☐	☐
Cabinets	☐	☐	☐
Countertop	☐	☐	☐
Counter Space	☐	☐	☐
Flooring	☐	☐	☐
Oven / Stove	☐	☐	☐
Microwave	☐	☐	☐
Layout	☐	☐	☐
Light Fixtures	☐	☐	☐
Backsplash	☐	☐	☐
Pantry	☐	☐	☐
Appliances	☐	☐	☐
Island	☐	☐	☐

	Good	Average	Poor
Basement	☐	☐	☐
Garage	☐	☐	☐

COMMUNITY

	Good	Average	Poor
Immediate Neighborhood	☐	☐	☐
Close to Employment	☐	☐	☐
Close to Shopping	☐	☐	☐
Close to Transportation	☐	☐	☐
Close to Schools / Daycare	☐	☐	☐
Close to Places of Worship	☐	☐	☐
Near Recreational Facilities	☐	☐	☐
Close to Airport	☐	☐	☐
Near Police and Fire Department	☐	☐	☐

Address ______________________ Price ______________

Bedrooms __________ Bathrooms __________ Sq.Ft. ______________

Lot Size: __________ Year Built __________ School District ________

Annual Tax __________

EXTERIOR

	Good	Average	Poor
View/Yard/Landscaping	☐	☐	☐
Trees	☐	☐	☐
Lawn (Front)	☐	☐	☐
Lawn (Back)	☐	☐	☐
Fences (condition)	☐	☐	☐
Landscaping (condition)	☐	☐	☐
Irrigation / Sprinkler	☐	☐	☐
	☐	☐	☐
House Type	☐	☐	☐
Exterior Siding	☐	☐	☐
Deck / Patio / Porch	☐	☐	☐
Garage	☐	☐	☐
Window / Doors	☐	☐	☐
Roof / Gutters	☐	☐	☐
Fencing	☐	☐	☐

HOME SYSTEMS

	Good	Average	Poor
Electrical	☐	☐	☐
Air Conditioning / Fans	☐	☐	☐
Heating	☐	☐	☐
Security	☐	☐	☐
Plumbing	☐	☐	☐
Intercom	☐	☐	☐

FEATURES

	Good	Average	Poor
Home Warranty	☐	☐	☐
Energy Saving Features	☐	☐	☐

INTERIOR

	Good	Average	Poor
Walls / Trim / Ceilings	☐	☐	☐
Flooring	☐	☐	☐
Stairs	☐	☐	☐
Storage	☐	☐	☐
Living Room	☐	☐	☐
Family Room	☐	☐	☐
Dining Room	☐	☐	☐

	Good	Average	Poor
Master Bedroom	☐	☐	☐
Bedroom 2	☐	☐	☐
Bedroom 3	☐	☐	☐
Bedroom 4	☐	☐	☐
Master Bathroom	☐	☐	☐
Bathroom 2	☐	☐	☐
Bathroom 3	☐	☐	☐
Bonus / Game Room	☐	☐	☐

	Good	Average	Poor
Kitchen	☐	☐	☐
Cabinets	☐	☐	☐
Countertop	☐	☐	☐
Counter Space	☐	☐	☐
Flooring	☐	☐	☐
Oven / Stove	☐	☐	☐
Microwave	☐	☐	☐
Layout	☐	☐	☐
Light Fixtures	☐	☐	☐
Backsplash	☐	☐	☐
Pantry	☐	☐	☐
Appliances	☐	☐	☐
Island	☐	☐	☐

	Good	Average	Poor
Basement	☐	☐	☐
Garage	☐	☐	☐

COMMUNITY

	Good	Average	Poor
Immediate Neighborhood	☐	☐	☐
Close to Employment	☐	☐	☐
Close to Shopping	☐	☐	☐
Close to Transportation	☐	☐	☐
Close to Schools / Daycare	☐	☐	☐
Close to Places of Worship	☐	☐	☐
Near Recreational Facilities	☐	☐	☐
Close to Airport	☐	☐	☐
Near Police and Fire Department	☐	☐	☐

Address ______________________ Price ____________

Bedrooms ________ Bathrooms ________ Sq.Ft. ____________

Lot Size: ________ Year Built ________ School District ______

Annual Tax ________

EXTERIOR

	Good	Average	Poor
View/Yard/Landscaping	☐	☐	☐
Trees	☐	☐	☐
Lawn (Front)	☐	☐	☐
Lawn (Back)	☐	☐	☐
Fences (condition)	☐	☐	☐
Landscaping (condition)	☐	☐	☐
Irrigation / Sprinkler	☐	☐	☐
	☐	☐	☐
House Type	☐	☐	☐
Exterior Siding	☐	☐	☐
Deck / Patio / Porch	☐	☐	☐
Garage	☐	☐	☐
Window / Doors	☐	☐	☐
Roof / Gutters	☐	☐	☐
Fencing	☐	☐	☐

HOME SYSTEMS

	Good	Average	Poor
Electrical	☐	☐	☐
Air Conditioning / Fans	☐	☐	☐
Heating	☐	☐	☐
Security	☐	☐	☐
Plumbing	☐	☐	☐
Intercom	☐	☐	☐

FEATURES

	Good	Average	Poor
Home Warranty	☐	☐	☐
Energy Saving Features	☐	☐	☐

INTERIOR

	Good	Average	Poor
Walls / Trim / Ceilings	☐	☐	☐
Flooring	☐	☐	☐
Stairs	☐	☐	☐
Storage	☐	☐	☐
Living Room	☐	☐	☐
Family Room	☐	☐	☐
Dining Room	☐	☐	☐

	Good	Average	Poor
Master Bedroom	☐	☐	☐
Bedroom 2	☐	☐	☐
Bedroom 3	☐	☐	☐
Bedroom 4	☐	☐	☐
Master Bathroom	☐	☐	☐
Bathroom 2	☐	☐	☐
Bathroom 3	☐	☐	☐
Bonus / Game Room	☐	☐	☐

	Good	Average	Poor
Kitchen	☐	☐	☐
Cabinets	☐	☐	☐
Countertop	☐	☐	☐
Counter Space	☐	☐	☐
Flooring	☐	☐	☐
Oven / Stove	☐	☐	☐
Microwave	☐	☐	☐
Layout	☐	☐	☐
Light Fixtures	☐	☐	☐
Backsplash	☐	☐	☐
Pantry	☐	☐	☐
Appliances	☐	☐	☐
Island	☐	☐	☐

	Good	Average	Poor
Basement	☐	☐	☐
Garage	☐	☐	☐

COMMUNITY

	Good	Average	Poor
Immediate Neighborhood	☐	☐	☐
Close to Employment	☐	☐	☐
Close to Shopping	☐	☐	☐
Close to Transportation	☐	☐	☐
Close to Schools / Daycare	☐	☐	☐
Close to Places of Worship	☐	☐	☐
Near Recreational Facilities	☐	☐	☐
Close to Airport	☐	☐	☐
Near Police and Fire Department	☐	☐	☐

www.ingramcontent.com/pod-product-compliance
Lightning Source LLC
Chambersburg PA
CBHW070807220526
45466CB00002B/581
9781656224910